brilliant

NLP
Workbook

NLP
Workbook

David Molden and Pat Hutchinson

Prentice Hall
Business
is an imprint of

Harlow, England • London • New York • Boston • San Francisco • Toronto • Sydney • Singapore • Hong Kong
Tokyo • Seoul • Taipei • New Delhi • Cape Town • Madrid • Mexico City • Amsterdam • Munich • Paris • Milan

PEARSON EDUCATION LIMITED

Edinburgh Gate
Harlow CM20 2JE
Tel: +44 (0)1279 623623
Fax: +44 (0)1279 431059
Website: www.pearsoned.co.uk

First published in Great Britain in 2010

Pearson Education is not responsible for the content of third party internet sites.

ISBN: 978-0-273-73743-8

British Library Cataloguing-in-Publication Data
A catalogue record for this book is available from the British Library

Library of Congress Cataloging-in-Publication Data
A catalog record for this book is available from the Library of Congress

10 9 8 7 6 5 4 3 2 1
14 13 12 11 10

Typeset in 10/14pt Plantin by 3
Printed by Ashford Colour Press Ltd, Gosport

Contents

Acknowledgements

We would like to convey our appreciation and recognise the contribution and influence of a number of NLP developers, and our own teachers including:

Richard Bandler
John Grinder
Lesley Cameron Bandler
Stephen Gilligan
Robert Dilts
Charles Faulkner
Wyatt Woodsmall
Stephen and Connirae Andreas
Gregory Bateson
Alfred Korzybski
Naom Chomsky
Robert Anton Wilson

Introduction – Welcome to the Brilliant NLP Workbook

How this book is different from Brilliant NLP

We wrote *Brilliant NLP* to give an insight to the subject with a range of practical exercises so readers could really experience NLP for themselves. The exercises in this workbook will take you systematically through a journey of self-discovery and personal change. Whether or not you have read *Brilliant NLP* (and it is recommended as an ideal 'first read' for new-comers to the topic), the exercises in this workbook will help you to access your inner resources and put you in control of your life.

What is NLP?

Neuro-linguistic programming (NLP) is an attitude of mind and a set of tools and techniques for getting the best possible result out of life, work and relationships. It reveals how your mind really works, and how you use it to make decisions and interact with the world around you. You could say that NLP tools give you the means to be successful in three key relationships:

1 with other people

2 with your work and other pursuits

3 with yourself.

The simplest way of describing NLP to someone with no knowledge or experience is with the metaphor of the frog living at the bottom of the well. As the frog looks up, he sees a small circle of sky and thinks this is all that exists in the world. Then one day the frog is hit by an overpowering curiosity to climb up the well and take a closer look at the small circle of light. As he arrives at the top of the well, he suddenly sees the vastness of the landscape extending in all directions and he thinks to himself, 'wow, what a lot of world to explore; why didn't I make this journey before today?'

Once you assimilate the attitudes of NLP and become confident with some of the techniques, you will suddenly see a much bigger world of possibilities to explore, and you may wonder, like the frog, why you never made this journey before. To try to explain this in real terms has little effect; it would be like trying to convince the frog who is still at the bottom of the well that there is a vast world to explore above the well. His experience tells him that the well is the entire world and he is unable to even conceive a vastness when all he sees from his perspective when he looks up is a small circle of light.

What you can do with NLP

You may have bought, borrowed or been given this book because you want a practical guide to using NLP, or you may be an NLP coach or trainer and want a reference guide to NLP material and exercises. We have designed and written this workbook with all these uses in mind and included many practical tips from our experience of training NLP and using it as coaches for the past 18 years.

NLP spans all areas of life and work. It can be used by all professions wherever there is a desire to succeed. There are techniques to remove barriers to success such as limiting beliefs and value conflicts, and there are techniques to develop the energy and drive to step up your game and achieve your most outrageous dreams and audacious goals. There are techniques to build self-confidence, positive motivation and drive, patience and other internal states. There are techniques for engaging groups and presenting to large audiences like an Obama or Mandela.

Maybe you want to change your diet or exercise regime, your job, your business, or just to get out of bed earlier in the morning. First you must know what is stopping you from taking action so you can deal with it and then create the motivation and energy to drive the change you desire.

Current state to desired state

The exercises in the book will assist you in moving from a 'current state' to a 'desired state'. Whether your current state is an internal emotional state, or a set of external circumstances, there are techniques which work on both. There are also universal models which help to move teams and organisations from their current state to a desired state. We encourage you to use the exercises in this book to create more desired states for yourself, the people you care about, and the people you work with.

We wish you every success!

How to use this book

This is a workbook, written to be used by anyone who wants to use NLP for their own personal development, or by NLP practitioners, trainers and coaches who want a reference book for their work with clients. As a practitioner, you may want to dip into a particular section for a specific exercise. If you are new to NLP, we suggest that you start at the beginning and work your way through so you grasp each NLP concept and build up your understanding step by step.

Brilliant overview

You will find an overview of what you will learn in each chapter under the heading 'Brilliant overview'.

Exercises

Some exercises are standard, classic NLP procedures; others have been modified by us, and some are designed to help you integrate the material in the book and apply it to your own circumstances. Some exercises have an added explanation of how they work, with pointers for practitioners and coaches who may be using them with their clients. We have called these two aspects 'solo' and 'duo', and the subject of the exercise is referred to as the 'explorer'.

Brilliant actions and brilliant tips

Quick tips and quick actions are included as stand-alone extras to stretch you and to supplement the main exercises. They are liberally placed throughout each of the chapters.

Brilliant presuppositions

NLP is based upon a set of presuppositions. These can be found in a chapter on their own as well as being spread throughout the book to support the various exercises.

Brilliant examples

You will get the most from this book by having some personal examples to work with. Where you see the heading 'Personal examples', it is an opportunity to choose something about your life you would like to change.

Index of exercises

This will enable you to find a specific exercise easily.

CHAPTER 1

Create
compelling
outcomes

Jeff's story

Jeff: 'I don't know what to do next.'

Chloe: 'Well, what are your options?'

Jeff: 'Oh, I don't know. I could become a gardener or a plumber or learn some other trade, or I might go into property. I could also take up a new hobby, but which one?'

Chloe: 'That's quite a list, Jeff. So which one are you likely to enjoy the most?'

Jeff: 'That's the trouble, I haven't a clue. All I know is that I don't want to do this kind of work any more. In fact, every decision I have made in my life has been decided on what I don't want. When I left college I didn't want to be poor and so I took the first decently paid job which came along, and I have followed that same pattern for the last 15 years.'

Chloe: 'Hmm, I see your dilemma, but have you never enjoyed your work, Jeff?'

Jeff: 'No, not really' he exclaimed. 'I only ever worked to avoid being poor.'

Chloe: 'Then finding something you can enjoy which will enrich your life seems a good place to begin. What do you think?'

Jeff: 'That would be magic.'

Whether making an important telephone call, implementing a two-year strategy, or moving on to the next stage in your life, if something within you is stopping you from getting on with it a compelling outcome will be useful. By compelling I mean that you have a real desire to get out of your bed, up from your sofa, or away from a dull job and get stuck in to something worthwhile with enthusiasm and conviction.

Compulsion helps where you really want to do something but you don't get off the starting block, or if you do the commitment is short-lived. To help make more of your outcomes compelling there is a set of conditions commonly referred to as 'well-formed'.

In this chapter you will learn how to create well-formed outcomes for the things you want to achieve and use the exercises to work through one or more specific achievements. You will also learn how enjoying what you do will make the journey of achievement easier to navigate and much more compelling.

The concept of outcomes is a central theme to NLP and will feature throughout the book. Having well-formed outcomes while you read this book will help you get the most from the exercises by increasing your drive to go for the things that are really fulfilling for you.

brilliant overview

You are about to learn:

- How to ensure that your outcomes are well-formed
- The dynamics of basic motivation
- Being clear about the outcome you want
- The enjoyment factor – how it works
- The importance of both internal and external resources
- Being in control; using initiative and taking responsibility
- How to check the ecology of your decisions using Cartesian logic
- Measuring your progress
- Planning for success.

▶ brilliant examples

Think of a situation you would like to change, or something you would like to achieve. It could be a phone call, a job interview, finding a partner, getting out of a relationship, starting a business, making a career change, learning a new skill or getting fit. Describe it under the relevant category below.

1 An aspect of your work.

_____

_____

_____

2 A relationship.

_____

_____

_____

3 Something about yourself that you would like to change.

_____

_____

_____

Keep your brilliant examples at the front of your mind as you progress through the chapter and as you complete each exercise your outcome will become well-formed.

☀ brilliant tip

It could be time to **stretch your horizons**. If you find yourself thinking of a change you want to make and you don't believe **you have it in you to succeed**, how will you know that **it's possible** if you don't even **take the first step?**

Basic motivation dynamics

A person can be motivated by pleasure or pain or to put it another way achievement or avoidance. When you line up both pleasure and pain with achievement and avoidance you create the driving forces for positive change. At a very basic level of human behaviour we are programmed to seek security and to avoid insecurity, so both these dynamics are part of our make-up. Sometimes these become unbalanced as a response to life experiences. In our story, Jeff had fallen into a habit of choosing work based upon criteria of avoiding poverty. Understanding how a habit works is more useful than knowing why it developed. Knowing *how* you create your habit is the first step to making a change, and changing habits is what NLP was designed for.

State your outcome in the positive

If I ask you not to think of a pink elephant, it's too late, you have already done so. You have to bring the object into your mind in order to know what not to think about. The mind is unable to represent a negative. Whether you think of something you want, or something you want to avoid, the mind creates an image and doesn't know how to negate it. This means that your mind can get easily confused between the things you want and the things you don't want. Whatever you focus on is likely to come your way. The more you think about 'not travelling', the more you find jobs with travelling involved, and the more disheartened you may become. The more you think about 'a local job' the more local jobs you will find.

Some people have a compulsion to do things which are not good for them, such as drinking too much alcohol, taking too many drugs, gambling, overeating. If you are going to have a compulsion, then why not make it something which is good for you, and good for others too? How about being compulsive about keeping healthy? Being nice to people? Being a great sales executive, socialising, philanthropy? Painting or writing? Being a terrific parent, partner or friend? Eating well? Imagine that each time you walk out of your front door, you have an inner compulsion to do something which is good for you. Imagine taking that compulsion to work with you, or to a social gathering. How might this change things for the better?

 **brilliant** action

Whenever you catch yourself describing something you want to avoid, ask yourself **'what do I want instead of this?'** State it in the positive and you are less likely to get what you want to avoid and more likely to **get what you really want**.

exercise 1.1　State your desired outcome in the positive

Take the desired change or achievement stated in your brilliant example and identify anything you want to avoid. Take each one and restate it in the positive.

What I want to avoid is:

_____

_____

_____

What I want instead is:

_____

_____

_____

The enjoyment factor

Forcing yourself to do a job you dislike, or becoming numb in a job with little fulfilment is a recipe for poor performance and stress. Staying in a relationship which has become stale will also create stress. When you enjoy what you do, or who you are with, it is easier to focus and concentrate since you are not so easily distracted.

Think also about the purpose of what you do. A task itself can be enjoyable, but one that leads to a tangible benefit of some sort is even more satisfying. It's more about the value of your contribution to a purpose which the task is designed to fulfil than the doing of the task alone.

 **brilliant** presupposition

'You have all the resources you need to succeed.'

This relates to internal resources of which you have all you are likely to need to accomplish anything. The questions to ask are, 'In what measure do you have the resource? 'Have you used it much lately?' 'Are you prepared to commit yourself to the challenge?'

Internal and external resources

Before you begin to take steps in the direction of your outcome, check if you have the resources you will need to accomplish it.

External resources consist of money, space, information, equipment, people and materials that you might require for any kind of project. You may need contacts that can put you in touch with people who have special knowledge or skills. You may want to hire a coach, attend a training course or enlist the services of a mentor.

exercise 1.2   External resources

Make a list of the external resources you need to achieve your outcome.

_____

_____

_____

_____

_____

Having identified the external resources you want, you need to know where you can acquire them. You may already know this, but if you don't, then find people who already have the resources you want and ask them how they went about getting them. You can learn so much from other people, and the more people you ask the more ideas and solutions you will find.

Internal resources are within you, and include such things as confidence, persistence, patience, determination and decision-making.

exercise 1.3 Internal resources

From the list below, identify the resources which you feel you will need in order to achieve your outcome and score each one out of 10 on how much of it you have now (0 = none; 10 = in abundance).

Internal resource	Need? Yes/No	Score 0–10
Confidence		
Patience		
Determination		
Persistence/tenacity		
Flexibility		
Decision-making		
Certainty		
Courage		
Focus and concentration		
Playfulness		
Motivation and drive		
Diplomacy		
Reflection		
Logic		
Other		
Other		
Other		

How to get the most out of this exercise

Solo. As the solo explorer, relax, sit back in your chair and exhale deeply. Bring to mind the outcome you want to achieve and imagine it is within your grasp. See a colourful image in your mind's eye of you making this happen and pay attention to your feelings as an indication of the resources you feel you will need.

Duo. As a practitioner or coach guiding the explorer through the exercise, be sure to give clear instructions to create the 'within your grasp' image. Be careful not to put words into the explorer's mouth, rather go with whatever the explorer comes up with. You are likely to need a good dose of patience yourself for this exercise, so allow long silences as the explorer turns feelings into words describing inner resources. If the explorer seems to be struggling, you can ask 'as you look at what is within your grasp, can you see anything missing that you feel you are going to need?' The explorer may also identify further external resources during this exercise, so just note them down.

How does this exercise work?

When you are reluctant to do something about a situation, or procrastinate in making a decision, the thoughts are often fleeting at best. The negative feelings which accompany the thoughts are unpleasant, and so there is a tendency to say, 'some other time' and get busy with something else. By staying focused on what you want, and staying in the feelings for longer than a fleeting moment it is more likely you will come up with the resources you need to make your desired outcome compelling.

Later in the book you will learn some techniques for creating the internal resources you have identified. At that point you will be reminded to return to this exercise, so for now relax and know that soon you will be increasing the scores you have just put down to 10 and beyond!

 **brilliant** tip

Inner resources are available to everyone. They are a combination of thinking and feeling in a particular way. Whatever you need, whether it's confidence, concentration or persistence, you can have as little or as much of it as you want.

Take initiative, be responsible, keep in control

Some people are passive observers of life. They like to sit back and allow others to take initiative. This is no place to be if you want to achieve something. Taking initiative means deciding for yourself, making decisions that are good for you, and following through on those decisions.

Having taken an initiative, a quick way to lose your motivation and drive is to give up because other people or events seem to be working against you. Whenever you blame external circumstances for not making progress, you have given up responsibility and handed both power and control over to those circumstances.

Responsibility could be written as 'response-ability' in recognition of your ability to do something about the circumstances which involve you. So when faced with a tough decision keep hold of the baton, get involved and do something about it. In this way you stay in control. When you recruit others to help you out, or ask friends for favours, if you sit back and trust that they will do as you have asked you have let go of control. With the best will in the world, other people juggle priorities just as much as you do, and things drop off their list. Make sure that you don't.

Checking the ecology of your decisions

Some people work so hard at being successful that they ignore, or just don't have time for other aspects of their life, family and relationships. Success in one area can bring unhappiness in another.

Before you embark on a courageous new life path, it's worth checking through the ecology of your decision. This means considering how your decision is likely to impact your relationships as well as the impact of not making it.

 **brilliant** presupposition

'If it's possible for one person it's also possible for others.'

Just make sure that you know what it is going to take for you to accomplish your goal, and how this will affect other aspects of your life and relationships.

One way of doing this is to run your outcome through an exercise of Cartesian logic. The four questions below test all possible consequences resulting from deciding either yes or no in relation to your outcome.

exercise 1.4   Ecology check

Answer each question below in relation to your brilliant examples and consider how the people you care about might be affected as well as the impact on you.

Q1 What will happen if I don't make this decision?

_____

_____

_____

Q2 What won't happen if I don't make this decision?

_____

_____

_____

Q3 What won't happen if I make this decision?

_____

_____

_____

Q4 What will happen if I make this decision?

_____

_____

_____

How to get the most out of this exercise

Solo. Spend a good few minutes on each question. Imagine what life may be like in each of the four scenarios, and check how you feel about each one. Which of the four scenarios feels more appealing to you? By the time you have answered all four questions you should be certain about the decision you are going to make. You may also have come up with some questions to ask other people about what they think of your decision.

Duo. As a practitioner or coach guiding the explorer through the exercise, make sure that enough time is spent on each one. Encourage the explorer to think of all the people who may be remotely affected by the decision whichever way it might go. Ask them to check the strength of feeling about their answers to each question.

Measuring your progress

Measuring progress sounds like basic common sense yet so many people get caught up in activities that do not provide a measurable return. Even planning a day out can go wrong if you don't know what you really want to get out of it.

Whether you want to have a fun day at the beach, a memorable anniversary dinner or a new business it pays to know what you want so you can measure whether or not you are achieving it.

 **action**

Find a friend to ask or go to an online forum and post the following request:
'I intend to achieve (X) outcome. What evidence would tell you that I had achieved my outcome?' Pay attention to what comes back.

Use sensory evidence

Sensory evidence is tangible; it's what you actually see and hear that tells you progress is being made. Here are some examples of how you would use sensory evidence in a number of different scenarios:

- *Building a business.* Increasing enquiries for your product or service; sales and profit figures; customer feedback.

- *Coaching a client.* Look for your clients' state growing increasingly congruent with their desired outcome and listen to what they say and the tone in which they say it. You are looking and listening for congruence between words, body language and voice tone.

- *Improving fitness.* Faster recovery time when exercising; being more flexible; feeling lighter/stronger/more relaxed; less effort required for certain activities like climbing stairs, riding your bike or walking uphill.

- *Motivating a team.* Meetings are more vibrant; people are asking questions and taking initiative; work-rate increases; problems are dealt with quicker; better decisions are made.

- *Finding a partner to share your life with.* Your partner says 'I enjoy being with you' in a congruent voice. Communication is both ways and frequent. You feel better about the relationship as each day goes by.

---

exercise 1.5   What to measure?

Take one of your brilliant examples and decide how you will measure the progress towards your desired outcome. Take your time and come up with some sensory evidence you can use to reliably measure your achievement.

What I will see is:

_____

_____

_____

What I will hear is:

_____

_____

_____

How I will feel is:

_____

_____

_____

How to get the most from this exercise

Solo. When you have found some evidence look at yourself from an observer's perspective and see if further evidence occurs to you. What evidence might an observer use to determine your degree of success?

Duo. As a practitioner or coach, help the explorer to evaluate each type of evidence. Test them by asking 'what will you see/hear exactly?' Be careful also to make a distinction between feelings of excitement and feelings which are caused by progress. People can easily get excited about their project and mistake these feelings for feelings of progress or success. Test by asking 'what is this feeling telling you?' or 'how does this feeling relate to your progress?'

 **brilliant** presupposition

'There is no failure, only feedback.'

Whatever you pursue, there will be feedback. The question is, are you receptive to it, are you measuring it, and are you adapting as a result?

Planning for success

Planning is about making sure you have your resources when you want them so you can achieve your outcome within a certain timeframe. Some people are very good at estimating how long things really take, and these people make good planners. Others are poor estimators of time and frequently allow too much or too little time to get things done. It all comes down to the value you put on time itself compared with the value you put on what you do with it. You will find exercises using time later in the book; here all you need to do is use a timeline, as described below, to put some substance into your outcome and bring it alive.

One way of planning is to write a list of what to do. Whilst this may work for simple outcomes like a shopping trip, it can be significantly improved upon for bigger or more complicated outcomes.

exercise 1.6   Visualise your timeline

When you think about a goal you look forward and imagine what you have to do to achieve it. This is fine, but there is a more effective and revealing approach. Imagine that you have already achieved your desired outcome, and then look back to see what you had to do to achieve it. To do this you are going to need a little space.

1   Place a marker on the floor to indicate the position of 'now'.

2   Stand on your marker and imagine a line on the floor extending in one direction. Look down this line and estimate how far down the line is the point at which you will have achieved your outcome. For example, a period of one year might be represented by three metres. There is no hard and fast rule about the ratio of space to time; it will just feel right.

3   Slowly walk down the line from 'now' and place a marker at this future point. Stand here looking back to your original marker in the 'now' position.

4   Imagine you have achieved your outcome. How does this feel? What can you see and hear? Take some time and really immerse yourself in the feeling of achievement.

5   Look back down the timeline and see all the things you had to do

in order to be successful. Relax and allow images and movies to run through your mind as you see the detail of each task, decision and interaction that moved you forward.

6   Can you see anywhere you needed a particular skill or other resource? What were the key challenges you faced?

7   Now get to it!

How to get the most from this exercise

Solo. As you stand in the future position looking back to 'now', make sure that any comments you make or questions you ask yourself are articulated in the past tense, i.e. 'what you **had** to do' rather than 'what you **have** to do'.

Duo. As a practitioner or coach, help the explorer by making sure they stay relaxed. Have them connect deeply with the feelings of success. If you are not convinced that they are enjoying the experience, ask if they have any doubts or fears about their outcome and deal with them before moving on. Check that their language remains in the past tense at all times when standing on the future marker. Help them to use their imagination by asking questions such as:

Q   **What can you see as you look back at what you had to do?**

Q   **What were the main challenges?**

Q   **How did you overcome them?**

How does this exercise work?

By physically laying out a timeline you are giving yourself space to visualise, and by imagining you have already succeeded you are tricking your mind into thinking that you have achieved your outcome. This all makes the journey ahead so much easier and adds a depth of clarity far greater than you can achieve through conventional pencil and paper planning. It's like having pseudo hindsight. The mind uses the same process to represent a past thought as it does a future thought – images, sounds, smells, tastes and feelings. So when you speak in the past tense and make your images bright and clear the mind codes these events as strong memories. Even though none of the activity has actually happened yet, and at a conscious level you know this, your mind represents it at a deeper level as if it has.

CHAPTER 2

Reprogramming your habits

Bernard's indecision

Bernard: 'It's so frustrating for me. Should I take the job in London, go for promotion here or look for a job with more responsibility?'

Debbie: 'Don't you enjoy what you are doing now?'

Bernard: 'I used to, but I feel I want a fresh challenge.'

Debbie: 'So are there no challenges for you here?'

Bernard: 'Possibly, but it just doesn't seem as exciting as some of the other options.'

Debbie: 'OK, so what do you see yourself achieving in the next five years?'

Bernard: 'I want to be a director making strategic decisions.'

Debbie: 'And how are you going to achieve this ambition if you don't commit yourself for long enough to make the grade?'

Bernard: 'Hmmm. Good question.'

Debbie: 'And what do you want to be making strategic decisions about?'

Bernard: 'To be honest I haven't really thought about this.'

Debbie: 'Well, isn't this important to you?'

Bernard's indecision was caused by his desire for difference and desire for choice which were creating an internal conflict. The more he pondered this, the more stressed he became. It might seem at first sight

▶

that Bernard's situation is easily resolved by choosing a new direction, but there is more to it than simply making a choice.

The drivers behind Bernard's conflict are often called thinking or motivation patterns. They begin their work at a deep unconscious level to determine your behaviour in a particular context. The technical term for these patterns is metaprogrammes, so called because like a computer program they hold the instructions which determine what the computer will do, and, like a computer, motivation patterns which don't get you great results can be re-programmed for success.

Metaprogrammes determine your general approach to life and they work in a similar way to your personal values. One way to think about them is as intrinsic values; they are so deeply rooted that they are intrinsic to your personality. In the story, Bernard was influenced by his tendency to seek fresh new challenges at certain intervals of time, and the closer he got to the next interval, the more indecisive and irrational about his choices he became.

brilliant overview

You are about to learn:

- How to identify your metaprogrammes
- Linking your strengths to certain metaprogrammes
- How to recognise which programmes are helping and which are hindering achievement of your outcomes
- The effect of some metaprogramme combinations
- How metaprogrammes affect your work
- How extreme behaviour can be explained by metaprogrammes
- How to change a metaprogramme.

▶ brilliant examples

Think of something you do which is not serving you well. It could be anything that hinders you from making the progress you would like to make. Sometimes a tendency to be silent or inactive can be as inhibiting as demonstrable behaviour. It could be the way you react to someone, or how you approach your work. You may not know exactly what the behaviour is, in which case just describe how it feels. Write it under the relevant category below.

1   An aspect of your work.

2   A relationship.

3   Something else you feel you are struggling to achieve.

Keep your examples at the front of your mind as you progress through the chapter. As you complete each exercise, you will gain a deeper insight into which programmes are hindering and which are helping.

☀ brilliant tip

If you feel that there is something acting as an obstacle to the pursuit of something important to you, first acknowledge the feeling, and then look for the behaviour pattern/s that could be creating the obstacle.

How to identify your metaprogrammes

There may be one, two, three or more metaprogrammes which are not serving you well. Most will be recognisable from the following description of 10 metaprogrammes and there will be combinations responsible for certain behaviour patterns. Each metaprogramme presents two opposite ways of thinking and you may have a preference for one over the other, or you may use a mix of both. Think of these opposites as being at opposing ends of a continuum where your preference can be shown as a range consisting of varying amounts of both.

Certain patterns of behaviour tend to repeat with consistency. These patterns play out at work, in family relationships and in social scenarios, although a person may demonstrate different patterns in each context. For example, a person may operate from one end of a continuum at work and from the opposite end in the context of family.

There is no 'normal range' relating to metaprogrammes. There is only difference, and so the question to ask is not whether a particular pattern is good or bad, right or wrong, but is it useful in a specific context? Remember that an extreme metaprogramme can be a strength as much as a weakness, and so the idea is not to put limits on a behaviour pattern but increase its opposite pattern to achieve balance and flexibility. Let's take them one at a time, and as you read through them keep in mind your brilliant examples.

1 Towards <–> Away from

Towards

Future oriented, thoughts focused on events that have not yet happened, wondering about the future. Excitement and enjoyment is about the future much more than reminiscing about the past. Optimistic outlook with an expectation that each new day will bring excitement. More proactive than reactive. Motivated by rewards for achievement.

Work

Will enjoy jobs with future targets to aim for, or where there are improvements to make or new systems/products/projects to design or implement. Works well where there are rewards for achievement and where risk is either tolerated or encouraged. Will not perform well in highly regimented and risk-averse cultures where the feeling of being frequently restrained is likely to lead to mental and physical stress.

Turned on by

Ideas and words such as go for it, achieve, success, drive forward, future, create.

Turned off by

Rules and regulations that limit them and prevent progress, red tape, bureaucracy, overly cautious people and systems, anything which holds them back. Pessimists and people who focus on problems.

How to notice this pattern

A person with a strong tendency for **towards** thinking will know what they want to achieve. If you ask them about their goals or ambitions they will be able to easily describe them to you. They may or may not have a set timescale in mind for a future goal, but they will be able to describe it to you. They will ask more questions about tomorrow, next week, month and year than questions about past events.

Away from

Cautious, thoughts focused on what to avoid. Prevention is the aim. If you know what the problems might be, you can prepare to avoid them. Wonders about problems, difficulties and the worst the day might bring. Pessimistic outlook with the expectation that each new day will bring problems to be avoided. More reactive than proactive. Motivated by avoidance of pain – the stick.

Work

Will enjoy jobs which require the creation of rules and regulations, safe working practices, contingency plans, terms and conditions, legal documents, bureaucracy. Will not perform well in high-risk cultures or where a high degree of initiative and proactivity are required.

Turned on by

Clear boundaries, written rules and regulations, knowing the pitfalls, safety, security, having certainty about the future, structure. Like to know what the future might hold so they can prepare to avoid anything unpleasant.

Turned off by

Surprises, the unknown, unpredictability, risk, gung-ho mentality, entrepreneurism, lack of rules and structure, people who break or ignore rules, anything which stops them from analysing potential problems.

How to recognise this pattern

A person with a strong tendency for **away from** thinking will know what they want to avoid. If you ask them about their goals or ambitions they are likely to tell you what it is they don't want to happen, and have difficulty describing exactly what they do want. In conversation they tend to focus on negative situations and possible problems.

In an organisation you typically find conflict between **Towards** oriented people who are happy taking risks, and **Away from** oriented people who prefer to play safe and work within a secure, predictable and controlled environment.

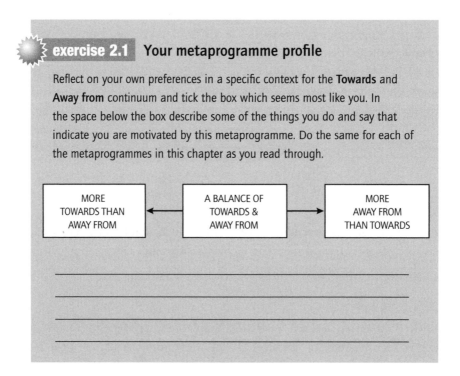

exercise 2.1   **Your metaprogramme profile**

Reflect on your own preferences in a specific context for the **Towards** and **Away from** continuum and tick the box which seems most like you. In the space below the box describe some of the things you do and say that indicate you are motivated by this metaprogramme. Do the same for each of the metaprogrammes in this chapter as you read through.

| MORE TOWARDS THAN AWAY FROM | ← | A BALANCE OF TOWARDS & AWAY FROM | → | MORE AWAY FROM THAN TOWARDS |

 **brilliant** tip

Invest time learning to think from whichever orientation you feel least attached to so that you develop a balanced flexibility across both thinking styles. Have more influence by adapting your language to respect the other person's personal orientation on this continuum.

2 Procedures <–> Options

Procedures

Likes to have a step by step procedure for getting things done. Enjoys logical sequences and will refer to manuals and handbooks which explain how to operate machines, gadgets, appliances, etc. Will always look for an established procedure.

Work

Following a plan. Anything with a set sequence of steps which can be followed. Practical tasks where the procedure is clear and requires little creative input. Highly structured environments with clarity of expectations. Is better at following procedures than creating them. Prefers to work with 'needs' more than 'possibilities'.

Turned on by

Lists, bullet points, tick boxes and agendas. Procedures manuals, how-to guides, tangible and practical tasks. Having a set of steps for completing tasks. Logical sequences. Knowing what has to happen when.

Turned off by

Ambiguity, lack of procedure, procedures which don't work very well, creative thinking, mind-mapping and brainstorming. Discussions which jump across unconnected topics.

How to recognise this pattern

A person with a strong tendency for **procedural** thinking will speak in a procedural way. They may count on their fingers, gesturing sequentially, e.g. 'we did this, and then we did this, now we have to do this', marking out a sequence with their hands as they speak. They use words like 'must, have to, need' rather than 'could, possibly, maybe'. They write in lists and like to use bullet points.

Options

Motivated by choice. Will generate alternative ways of approaching tasks. Likes to brainstorm and think creatively. Finds new ways to do existing tasks. Prefers to work intuitively than follow a set procedure. When faced with a decision will find a range of options from which to choose, but may procrastinate over the decision. This is because of the tendency to try to keep all options open. Can flit from one subject to another easily. May begin more projects than can be managed. Is better at writing procedures than following them.

Work

Will enjoy jobs which require creative thinking. Wants autonomy and the freedom to choose how to do something. Is comfortable with ambiguity and may totally ignore procedures. Is motivated by possibilities and freedom of choice.

Turned on by

Options, choices, alternatives, possibilities. Freedom to act in the moment and find new ways of getting things done. Like to work things out for themselves. Mind maps and creative thinking. More interested in the relationships between things and people than structural connections.

Turned off by

Control, structure and rigid procedure. Dislikes being told what must be done and how to do it. Lists, tick boxes, bullet-points, procedures manuals and handbooks. Detailed job descriptions.

How to recognise this pattern

A person with a strong tendency for **options** thinking will talk about possibilities, choices and use words like maybe, perhaps. They like to keep their options open and may even write in a diary in pencil so the appointment can be changed if something better comes along. In extreme cases, this pattern can lead to procrastination and lack of commitment. Gestures are circular and expansive in stark contrast to the more linear gestures of the **procedural** thinker.

In an organisation you typically find conflict between procedures oriented people and options oriented people. In an extreme case a procedural orientation can place a higher value on the procedure than what it is designed to achieve, and so fixing a broken procedure becomes the achievement itself.

Reflect on your own preferences in a specific context for the **Procedures** and **Options** continuum and tick the box which most seems like you. In the space below the box describe some of the things you do and say that indicate you are motivated by this metaprogramme.

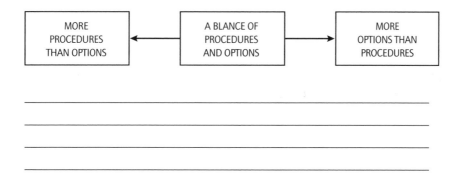

| MORE PROCEDURES THAN OPTIONS | ← → | A BLANCE OF PROCEDURES AND OPTIONS | ← → | MORE OPTIONS THAN PROCEDURES |

_____

_____

_____

_____

brilliant tip

The challenge with any team is to utilise the strengths of both orientations. To get things done requires both creativity and procedure. The challenge is twofold: 1) know when it is useful to leave the confines of a procedure and generate options, 2) learn how to create procedures which offer choice.

3 Internal reference <-> External reference

Internal reference

This is about making judgements and evaluations. How you know if something is right, wrong, good, bad or any other evaluation is based on an internal reference. A person with a strong internal reference pays more attention to their own experience and feelings than any external reference and they may even ignore data which contradicts their own judgement.

Work

Will be suited to jobs where there is little external data and feedback and where decisions need to be made based on subjective experience. They tend to be poor at customer service because they value their own judgement more than customer feedback. Managers with this pattern may not see the value in giving their employees feedback since they do not require it themselves.

Turned on by

People who agree with them. Autonomy to make decisions based on own evaluation. People who are self-sufficient and can manage with minimal supervision and input from them.

Turned off by

Other people's opinions which differ from their own. Too much reliance on external data. People who need frequent feedback or instruction.

How to recognise this pattern

A person with a strong tendency to reference internally will use the words 'I', 'me' and 'my' much more than 'we' and 'our' even when making comments on behalf of a group or team, e.g. 'I think xxx', 'it doesn't work for me', 'I'm not convinced', 'it's not my responsibility'.

External reference

Makes judgements and evaluations based on external data and evidence. Requires validation from external sources. Will put effort into searching for evidence when there is a perceived lack of reliable information. Will frequently ask others what they think. Gives feedback to others whether they ask for it or not.

Work

Suited to jobs where research and external data collection are used to make decisions. Excellent at customer service roles especially customer facing because they sincerely want to understand the customer experience. Likely to become stressed in situations where no reliable external data is available, or where feedback is not valued.

Turned on by

Feedback about their performance. Data which helps them do their job better, or make better decisions. Statistics, charts, research, polls, focus groups.

Turned off by

A lack of meaningful data or evidence. People who shoot from the hip with no apparent external reference to justify their actions. Managers who don't give feedback. People who ignore or devalue external data or research.

How to recognise this pattern

A person with a strong tendency to use external references for evaluation will frequently ask other people what they think, or to describe their experience. They may belong to a number of different groups and get involved in networks which provide them with information on their special interests. They give feedback to anyone if they believe it will help in some way.

Whenever you come across excellent customer service, it is highly likely that external referenced managers are running the business. All too often, especially in financial services and technology companies, the level of customer satisfaction is poor due to internally referenced managers controlling the business and ignoring feedback from customers.

Reflect on your own preferences in a specific context for the **Internal reference** and **External reference** continuum and tick the box which most seems like you. In the space below the box describe some of the things you do and say that indicate you are motivated by this metaprogramme.

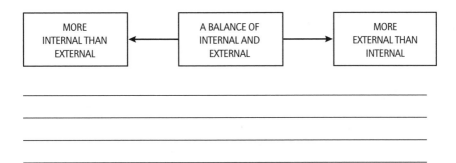

_____

_____

_____

_____

 **tip**

If you want an internally referenced person to accept your idea, put it in this way: '**You know** that it's crucial we improve customer service. Your support for the X project is the best way to achieve this, and **you know** we have to act fast.' The words that have the desired effect are in bold. To gain support from an externally referenced person you need to quote external data, research, and eminent people in the field who agree with you.

4 Global <–> Detail

Global

Likes to think about the big picture rather than the details of a topic, plan or idea. Concepts and principles are far more interesting than the nuts and bolts of how things work. Happier brainstorming for ideas than working out a plan of action. Likes to merge small things into a bigger entity, concept or category.

Work

Will enjoy a role which requires focus on strategy. Is able to relate well to strategic purpose, goals and aims of the organisation, and engaging in high level discussions. Is most effective in a competitive context when used with the external reference pattern. In contrast, it may be a liability when used with the internal reference pattern, as high-level decisions would be made on feelings rather than data and evidence.

Turned on by

Brainstorming, concepts, ideas, big picture. People who can hold a discussion at this high level. Challenges that require analysis of concepts and big ideas.

Turned off by

Details. People who bring up details in a plan, argument or idea. Challenges which require the frequent checking of details.

How to recognise this pattern

A person with a strong tendency for global thinking is likely to make cloud-concept drawings and mind-maps to illustrate their thinking. In conversation they talk about how things are related, or connected, or what they mean. They scale-up conversation and talk in brief sound bites. They often make errors in spelling and punctuation because the message is more important than the detail of how it is written. Numbers may be inaccurate. They may prefer to work with ball-park numbers than conduct an accurate assessment. Messages may be brief and general, causing confusion among people who like to have details.

Detail

Enjoys revelling in the details. Much happier with tangible things which can be measured and accounted for rather than ideas, theories and concepts. Quick to break things down into small parts. Like to dissect and disassemble.

Work

Will perform well in a role requiring focus on detail. Is able to easily spot errors, exceptions at a detail level. Is able to concentrate on the small details of a plan, process or project for long periods of time. Is also capable of being consumed by detail and missing the bigger picture of purpose, aims and goals. This thinking style does not make a good people manager. If promoted into a position where they are managing others, they may become micro-managers, frequently meddling in the details and unable to fully delegate responsibility.

Turned on by

People who can break down large ideas or tasks into small components. Activities which immerse them in the details.

Turned off by

Intangible ideas and concepts. Activities which offer no details. People who generalise and ignore or hold back detail.

How to recognise this pattern

A person with a strong tendency for detailed thinking asks for details when taking instruction or directions. They talk about their experience at a detail level and, as a consequence, they tend to take much longer than global thinkers to get their point across. There is often frustration when talking with a global thinker because they never get enough detail from them. Global thinkers may be frustrated at the tedium of detail and length of time a detail thinker needs to fully articulate their ideas.

Reflect on your own preferences in a specific context for the **Global** and **Detail** continuum and tick the box which most seems like you. In the space below the box describe some of the things you do and say that indicate you are motivated by this metaprogramme.

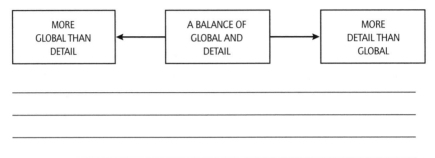

_____

_____

_____

_____

5 Self <–> Others

Self

Considers own needs before the needs of others. May not be aware of others' needs at all unless explicitly stated. Is unlikely to notice signals from a person's body language and tone of voice which may indicate they are uneasy or uncomfortable about something. Can easily perceive other people as 'getting in the way', e.g. other drivers, people in front them in a queue, anyone who causes them to be inconvenienced.

Work

They can put this thinking style to a useful purpose if they realise that they can achieve their goals by helping and supporting others to achieve their own. Otherwise, they may come across as uncaring and self-absorbed. They don't make good managers or leaders since they think more about themselves than their teams.

Turned on by

People who do things for them without being asked.

Turned off by

Needy high maintenance people.

How to recognise this pattern

A person with a strong tendency for self thinking is likely to use the word 'I' frequently in conversation. When in groups, they will cater to their own needs and leave others to cater for themselves. As a host, they may even say 'the drinks are over there, you can help yourself'.

Others

Cares about the needs of others before their own. Thinks about others, how they feel, what they need, how to make them happy, comfortable, successful. Likes other people to be happy, satisfied and successful and will go out of their way to help them.

Work

Ideally suited to customer-facing roles where customer service and satisfaction is required. Can make excellent trainers and coaches as long as they are able to look after their own needs. They are not so good at running businesses because they can give too much for too little return. In the extreme this thinking style can become problematic through inaction or withholding information, e.g. 'I didn't do/say anything because I didn't want to upset them'. They may go along with projects and initiatives simply to support the person responsible and help them to succeed. They do not like to ask for help with their own tasks as to do so would inconvenience the other person. They may spend so much time helping others that they neglect their own responsibilities.

Turned on by

People who ask for help and assistance. The feeling of having helped someone to achieve something or avoid an unpleasant situation.

Turned off by

People who ignore or seem unconcerned about the needs of others.

How to recognise this pattern

A person with a strong tendency for others thinking is likely to be asking other people if they need help. They are easily distracted by people around them who seem to be struggling with a task or decision and may offer assistance. They like to make tea/coffee for the group, leaving themselves until last and will generally help by opening doors and offering others who seem in a hurry their place in a queue.

Reflect on your own preferences in a specific context for the **Self** and **Others** continuum and tick the box which most seems like you.

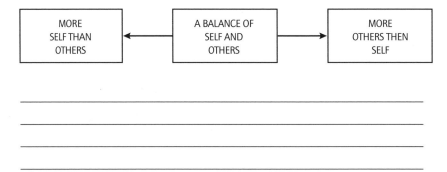

_____

_____

_____

_____

6 Independent <–> Cooperative

Independent

Likes to have full responsibility for their work and is uneasy when others are involved. Likes to focus on their work and be left alone while working. Ideally they like to have a working space where they will not be interrupted. May be very unproductive in busy open plan office environments due to ongoing distractions around them.

Work

They prefer jobs where they can retain overall responsibility from beginning to end. They are uneasy with shared responsibility and like to be in total control of the job. They can be valuable team players as long as meetings are planned and don't take up too much of their time.

Turned on by

Working alone away from distractions. People who acknowledge their need for personal space and personal time.

Turned off by

Noisy environments, office chatter, interruptions to their work especially if they are not important at that time, shared responsibility. They dislike having to wait for other people.

How to recognise this pattern

A person with a strong preference for an independent thinking style likes to have their own personal space and at meetings may sit at a slight distance from the people next to them. In groups they find an open space to occupy. They are happier having a discussion with one or two people than with a larger group, although in a larger group they may stand at the outer edge. They get frustrated when their concentration is broken by interruptions.

Cooperative

Likes to be in a group of people, ideally as a team with common aims. Enjoys open plan office environments and can work happily in busy, noisy environments. They need the stimulation of other people around them and will seek out other people to talk to. They are very happy sharing responsibility with others and they make excellent team players.

Work

They make very good networkers as they enjoy interacting with people in groups. Very productive in dynamic working environments where there are distractions from other people. They adapt well to training and coaching roles. They dislike jobs where they have to sit in one place for long periods of time.

Turned on by

Team activity in close proximity. Busy and active environments with frequent opportunities to talk with other people. Networking events and team meetings.

Turned off by

Being forced to work in isolation. Being unable to communicate face-to-face on a frequent basis. People who are reluctant to join in conversations.

How to recognise this pattern

A person with a strong preference for a cooperative thinking style is active, mobile, rarely settling in one place or position for very long. They like to chat, ask questions and generally interact frequently with other people.

Reflect on your own preferences in a specific context for the **Independent** and **Cooperative** continuum and tick the box which most seems like you. In the space below the box describe some of the things you do and say that indicate you are motivated by this metaprogramme.

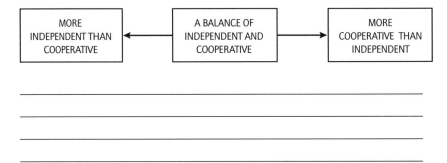

_____

_____

_____

_____

7 In-time <–> Through-time

In-time

Very focused in the moment with their full attention. Able to concentrate on the matter in hand without being distracted by thoughts of the immediate past and future. Because of this they usually have a poor judgement of the passing of time: 10 minutes easily turns into 30 minutes and an hour can turn into two and a half hours. They may plan ahead but very soon find themselves behind schedule as they consume more time than they had estimated. They are poor planners and may be regularly late for appointments.

Work

Suited to jobs that require thinking on the feet and unplanned reactive responses. Not so good at working to a detailed and defined plan. Like to be given jobs that need doing without delay.

Turned on by

Being able to fully engage with current activity. Being able to do things immediately.

Turned off by

Planning schedules, time management organisers, work that requires future scheduling. People who put great emphasis on timings and fixed plans.

How to recognise this pattern

They are often a few minutes late for meetings, may make an apology then relax into the meeting. They may not be fully prepared. They may rush away at the end to get to their next appointment. They act as though time is an unlimited resource. They rarely use professional organisers, preferring to keep a simple diary and notebook. Conventional time management courses have little effect on them.

Through-time

Split attention across immediate past/present/immediate future. Being on time and prepared for a future event is important. They may appear distracted as they focus their attention away from the matter in hand and on to their next appointment. Time is valuable and to be respected, so having plans and schedules is important so you can get the most from the time available. Don't waste time.

Work

They make good planners and project managers. They like to have time to plan and prefer proactivity to reactivity. Strong at sequencing tasks and preparing resources for future activities.

Turned on by

Schedules, plans and timed agendas. Knowing what they will be doing when. People who respect their time and use it efficiently. Sophisticated organisers and time management systems.

Turned off by

Having to wait for people. Having too little time to prepare. Disorganised people. People who leave things to the last minute. Lack of agenda and schedule.

How to recognise this pattern

People with a strong preference for through-time thinking will be punctual, or if they are late they will apologise profusely. They like to keep a tidy and organised record of meetings and tend to ask questions and make statements which refer to past and future activities. They enjoy time management courses but don't need them as they are naturally effective at managing their time.

Reflect on your own preferences in a specific context for the **In-time** and **Through-time** continuum and tick the box which most seems like you.

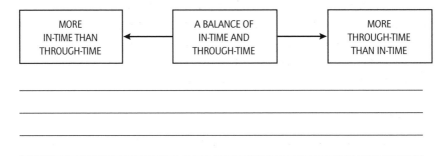

_____

_____

_____

_____

8 Sameness <–> Difference

Sameness

Likes established routines and familiar environments. When comparing new experiences or ideas their focus is on what is similar to existing experience or ideas. They look for similarities to what they already know. They are likely to stay in the same job for many years and socialise with the same group of friends for life. They may take the same holiday every year and have a fixed routine for domestic and social activities.

Work

Suited to jobs which do not change, or change only slightly over time, and have a high degree of consistency. They tend to enjoy jobs in quality control where they can easily spot variations to a standard and where there are standard routines.

Turned on by

Familiarity and routine. Knowing that each day and week will be much the same as the previous one. Familiar people in familiar places.

Turned off by

Change that affects their routine in any way. People who like to change things from systems and processes to office layouts, furniture and timings. Having to continually learn new systems. The thought of having their established routine disrupted.

How to recognise this pattern

A person with a strong tendency for sameness is very consistent in their day-to-day activities and may show signs of stress when forced to adapt and change. They resist change until it becomes inevitable or until they can avoid it no longer.

Difference

They create and drive change. They like to have variety and will create it even when unnecessary. They will find different ways to do things even when there is an established procedure. They have a low threshold for boredom and will leave a job when it ceases to offer sufficient variety. They tend to be inconsistent and will change their mind easily if a different idea takes their fancy. They are happy to be thrown into unfamiliar situations with little preparation.

Work

Well suited to jobs which offer variety and require ongoing development and change. Can work with a high degree of autonomy but may need to have their efforts directed so that change doesn't become chaos. Happy to continue learning new systems and processes. They make good generalists and often lack the consistency and longevity of focus to become expert in any one thing.

Turned on by

People who offer alternatives. Brainstorming. Generating new processes, procedures and systems for other people although they are unlikely to follow them with any degree of consistency.

Turned off by

Routine, procedure, rules and regulations. People who state rules and procedures and people who resist change.

How to recognise this pattern

People who have a strong preference for difference like to have their fingers in many pies and spread themselves widely in order to have variety. They are inconsistent in their approach to tasks and may change their mind in an instant if something appeals to them.

Reflect on your own preferences in a specific context for the **Sameness** and **Difference** continuum and tick the box which most seems like you.

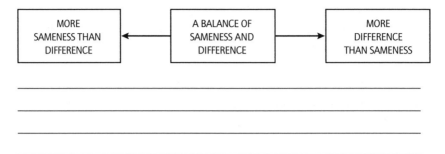

_____

_____

_____

_____

9 Doing <–> Considering

Doing

Action oriented. They like to get on with things and keep busy. They don't need fully thought out plans, preferring to get stuck in and work things out as they go along. They like to deal with things as they come up rather than leave decisions hanging in the air.

Work

Well suited to jobs requiring fast decisions. Will drive growth and progress when appropriately focused. Make effective senior managers including CEOs whose job is to drive progress and growth.

Turned on by

Quick decisions. Action-oriented people. Dynamic team environments.

Turned off by

Ditherers and procrastinators. Being held back from action. Waiting for a decision.

How to recognise this pattern

A person with a strong preference for action will be busy most of the time. They will not stay in one place for very long. When forced to spend time thinking about a potential activity they may show signs of frustration. They do not sit around thinking, preferring to be on the move. The sense of movement and action gives them a feeling of achievement.

Considering

Likes to think things through fully before making a decision and committing to action. Enjoys having time to thoroughly analyse the ins and outs of a strategy, plan or initiative.

Work

Enjoys analysis and likes to have plenty of time to think through all the implications of an initiative before making a decision. Can work well in project teams if given clear concrete timescales for decision-making. In extreme cases this thinking style can lead to procrastination where there are no externally set deadlines for decisions to be made.

Turned on by

Being given plenty of time to consider all angles. People who also like to discuss implications and think things through thoroughly.

Turned off by

Headstrong people who shoot from the hip. Fast decision-making. Being asked to make a decision with less time than they consider adequate to make a smart informed choice.

How to recognise this pattern

People with a strong preference for considering spend long periods of time sitting and thinking. They ask questions about what has and hasn't been taken into consideration. They frequently make comments like 'I want to think about this'.

Reflect on your own preferences in a specific context for the **Doing** and **Considering** continuum and tick the box which most seems like you.

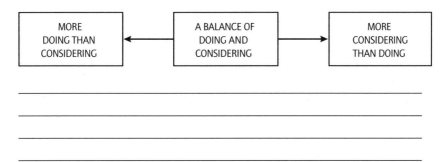

_____

_____

_____

_____

10 Thinking <–> Feeling

Thinking

A cerebral, logic and rational way of processing information and decision-making. Calm, analytical and emotionally dissociated from events.

Work

People with this preference tend to enjoy controlled, formal environments like finance, insurance and technology companies.

Turned on by

Rational discussion, discipline and controlled environments. Effective thinkers. The opportunity to analyse situations before making decisions. Decisions based on logical analysis.

Turned off by

Emotional displays. People who use gut feel and intuition. Proposals which are not backed up with evidence and data.

How to recognise this pattern

Controlled body language. Lack of emotional expression. Uses the word 'think' rather than 'feel', e.g. 'what do you think?'

Feeling

Expression of feelings using body language, gesture and voice tone as part of their verbal message. Use of feelings to evaluate propositions and decide what to do. Intuitive decision-making.

Work

Prefers informal environments which are not too tightly controlled. Likes to be animated in meetings and discussions.

Turned on by

Recognition of emotional states, e.g. 'it's important that people are happy in their work'. People who show how they feel, and who express themselves emotionally.

Turned off by

Cool-headed analytical people. Anyone who disregards or ignores an expressed emotion.

How to recognise this pattern

A person with a strong preference for feeling shows how they feel outwardly. Body language, gesture, voice tone, skin colour, lip size, pupil dilation are all indicators of emotion. The emotional range of the feeling person is far greater than that of the thinking person.

Reflect on your own preferences in a specific context for the **Thinking** and **Feeling** continuum and tick the box which most seems like you. In the space below the box describe some of the things you do and say that indicate you are motivated by this metaprogramme.

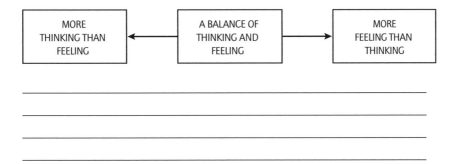

_____

_____

_____

_____

Linking your strengths to certain metaprogrammes

Your metaprogrammes will have an overriding influence on what you do well and what you don't do so well. There will be things you feel very comfortable doing and things you really dislike doing because they go against a fundamental metaprogramme. You may not even be conscious of what it is that causes the discomfort. On the other hand, it could be that someone else does something really well and you wish you were able to 'be like them'. If your self-esteem has taken a battering for some reason, you may even talk to yourself negatively about the things that others can do that you don't believe you can do.

---

exercise 2.2   The impact of metaprogrammes

Make three lists as follows:

List 1 – things I do well

In the table below write a list of all the things you do well. Be specific and count everything even if it's doing the shopping or cleaning your shoes. Next to each item write down the metaprogramme you think drives your success in these activities.

Things I do well	Metaprogramme driving my success

List 2 – things I don't do so well

Now do the same for the things you don't do so well. Remember to be specific. Think about the metaprogramme profile that would be most appropriate for achieving this task. For example, would a procedural pattern help you out?

Things I don't do so well | Which metaprogramme would be more likely to help me succeed?

_____

_____

_____

_____

_____

_____

_____

_____

List 3 – things I would like to do well

Write down the things you see other people do and would like to be able to do yourself. Be specific and write down the metaprogramme profile you think would be useful for each item. For example, 'always remembers people's birthdays' could be 'others, through-time and procedure'.

Things I would like to do well | Metaprogramme combinations that would help me to succeed.

_____

_____

_____

_____

_____

_____

_____

By now you will be seeing a pattern emerging whereby the stronger meta-programmes are influencing what you do well and what you don't do so well. Take some time to reflect on the areas where you would like to increase your flexibility. Later in the book we will show you how to model the strategies of people who do things you would like to be able to do. For now, start to notice your metaprogrammes in action and notice when they are hindering you and when they are helping you to achieve your outcomes.

Metaprogramme combinations

Some metaprogrammes combined together can either reinforce each other or balance each other out.

---

exercise 2.3   Metaprogramme combinations

Solo. By all means do this exercise alone – remember that by doing so you are limited to your own perception.

Duo. Choose someone who knows you well to discuss your answers with so that you get another perspective on your behaviour, your strengths and areas where more flexibility would be useful to you.

Write down what you think the effect of each of these combinations will be? Do you know anyone who may have these particular patterns? If you think a particular combination fits your own behaviour, then put a tick in the box on the right of the heading.

1 *Away from* with *External reference*   ☐

_____

_____

_____

2 *Considering* with *Options*   ☐

_____

_____

_____

3 *Options* with *Doing*   ☐

_____

_____

_____

4 *Procedures* with *Specifics*   ☐

_____

_____

_____

5 *Towards* with *Generalities*   ☐

_____

_____

_____

6 *Internal reference* with *Procedures*   ☐

_____

_____

_____

7 *External reference* with *Specifics*   ☐

_____

_____

_____

8 *Procedures* with *Through-time*   ☐

_____

_____

_____

9 *Procedures* with *Generalities*   ☐

_____

_____

_____

▶

10 *Internal reference* with *Doing*   ☐

_____

_____

_____

Here are some possibilities:

1 *Away from* with *External reference* – a tendency to filter for negative feedback resulting in low self-esteem.

2 *Considering* with *Options* – a recipe for procrastination as every option will need to be considered.

3 *Options* with *Doing* – the doing pattern here can act as a balance to the options; the need for action will overtake the desire for options at some point.

4 *Procedures* with *Specifics* – can be a recipe for being pedantic and inflexible.

5 *Towards* with *Generalities* – Likely to have big ideas and drive towards them. May not always see them through.

6 *Internal reference* with *Procedures* – a bit of a sergeant major – believes he knows what to do and his way is best.

7 *External reference* with *Specifics* – uses external measurement to assess success of a detailed approach. Such perfection could hinder progress.

8 *Procedures* with *Through-time* – well organised and planned. May not be able to cope when things don't go according to plan.

9 *Procedures* with *Generalities* – a bit of an idealist, sees only one big picture solution.

10 *Internal reference* with *Doing* – action man who appears to know what he is doing and doesn't consider opinions of others.

Extremes of both individual and combinations of patterns can produce extreme behaviours.

> **exercise 2.4** **Observing patterns of behaviour**
>
> Over the next few days take a look around you and watch people's behaviour. Note down anything which you think may be the result of extreme metaprogramme preferences. Notice the patterns people follow which might suggest certain metaprogramme combinations.
>
> _____
>
> _____
>
> _____
>
> _____
>
> _____
>
> _____

How metaprogrammes affect your work

Some roles lend themselves to certain metaprogramme preferences. For example, accountants and bankers will probably thrive on a procedural, detail pattern. Customer service people do well if they have External reference, Others patterns, and marketing people generally veer towards Options and Difference.

If you are in a role that suits your metaprogramme profile, you are likely to thrive and enjoy your work. Learning to be flexible will help you to communicate with and influence people from other areas of the business and with internal and external clients. If, however, your role works against your natural profile, you are more likely to become frustrated and unhappy. You may, however, be unaware of the cause of your frustration, so make sure you do the exercises in this chapter thoroughly, paying particular attention to any patterns which may go against your role.

How to balance a metaprogramme

Sometimes it is useful to introduce more balance into your metaprogramme profile, particularly if you would like to have more influence over those around you. For example, if you know you are extreme on the

Through-time pattern, you may find it difficult to relax in the here and now. If you are high on Procedures, you may find it difficult to accept new ways of doing things when people introduce new ideas. If you are high on Away-from, you are unlikely to take the risk necessary to move on in your role or life unless things become very uncomfortable for you.

Remember that your pattern will serve you well in some contexts so this is not about changing your pattern, rather gaining a better balance by increasing your flexibility and allowing you to behave differently in contexts where the pattern doesn't serve you so well. Now you have the awareness, you are almost there.

Here are some ways you could balance your patterns:

- Find someone who has the pattern you would like and 'model' the way they think and behave. Later on in this book you will learn how to model in more detail.
- Find yourself an NLP coach who will help you identify specific examples and select the appropriate techniques to help you increase your flexibility.
- Use the new behaviour generator described below.

exercise 2.5   New behaviour generator

1 Look down and ask yourself what if would be like if you were to take on this new behaviour.

2 Look up and create a framed picture of you doing the new behaviour. Take time to put in all the detail.

3 Make the picture big and bright and bring it closer towards you.

4 Mentally step into the picture and assess your feelings. Are these similar to the feelings you have experienced in the past when you have done something successfully? If the answer is 'yes', then you have completed the exercise. If not, then go back to your created picture, identify what is missing and repeat the exercise from this point until you recognise the feelings of success.

5   Repeat the exercise five to six times until the mental image is strong in your mind's eye, and the feelings are positive towards the new behaviour you are imagining.

Solo. This is a straightforward exercise to do on your own. Learn the process first and make sure your picture is clear and bright. Use a voice tone which suggests curiosity and discovery.

Duo. Help the explorer to stay in the process by giving clear directions at each stage, e.g., 'make the picture bigger', 'put a frame around it', 'put in the detail' 'intensify the colour', 'bring the picture forward'.

CHAPTER 3

Swap old
feelings for new

Paul's problem

Paul: 'I have a problem', said Paul with a sigh of desperation.

Joshua: 'Give it to me and I'll get rid of it for you', replied Joshua as he held out his hand to receive it.

Paul: 'No, you don't understand. I really do have a problem', insisted Paul.

Joshua: 'If you can't put it in my hand, then it can't exist other than in your head. Outside your head there are only circumstances; it takes a human mind to conjure up something we have learned to call a problem.'

Paul: 'But it's still my problem', insisted Paul.

Joshua: 'Yes it is, and you have probably imagined all kinds of circumstances for your problem. I expect you are telling yourself that you have this problem, and you know it's a problem because you feel so bad when you imagine it in this way, isn't that so?'

Paul: 'Yes, that's exactly how it is.'

Joshua: 'Good', said Joshua. 'As you find it so easy to imagine a problem, then you can simply imagine it to be something else which will make you feel better. When you feel better you will be in a better state to do something positive about the circumstances you have been calling a problem.'

f you have ever wondered how two people can look at the same circumstances and experience something different, you are about to learn how they do it. Life is full of examples. Take a group of four people who go on a long bus journey together. One person keeps complaining about the other drivers on the road, the second person worries about safety, the third is concerned about being late, and the fourth goes to sleep. They are all on the same car journey but having very different experiences.

Many people go through the day reacting to circumstances as if they had no choice, attributing the way they feel to whatever is going on around them. Not everyone does this. Some people have learned that the way they feel is a choice regardless of the circumstances. They seem to have more control over their emotions and as a consequence they appear happy, are able to focus, concentrate and enjoy themselves. As a result, their level of stress is far lower than that of people who feel they have no choice. Whether you imagine things to be one way or another, it is merely a construct which exists only in your mind. You can easily change this construct and swap feelings you would rather not have with ones that make you feel brilliant.

brilliant overview

You are about to learn:

- How you construct your response to events
- How your representation systems create your inner map of the outside world
- How your inner representation creates your feelings
- How to work with representations to rapidly change the way you feel
- How to read eye accessing cues which reveal how you process information
- How to collapse negative feelings which are anchored to certain events
- How to use anchoring to give you more control over your feelings.

▶ brilliant examples

Think of a situation which tends to generate negative feelings. Choose one which happens often such as:

1 An aspect of your work which you dislike, make mistakes with or struggle to complete.

_____

_____

_____

2 Another person who aggravates or frustrates you.

_____

_____

_____

3 Something about yourself that you don't like, maybe how you act in a situation, or a physical characteristic.

_____

_____

_____

☀ brilliant tip

There is no magic wand you can use to control another person, but you can learn to control yourself. If you feel stuck in one way of reacting, you can learn to react differently and make the new reaction stick. This in turn will cause the other person to react differently.

Your outcome

Identify what you want to change and describe it as an outcome by answering the questions below.

How would you like to experience this in the future?

_____

_____

_____

How would you like to feel about it?

_____

_____

_____

What positive results will this have for you?

_____

_____

_____

What other positive consequences are likely to happen?

_____

_____

_____

What else could come from making this change?

_____

_____

_____

Keep your brilliant examples and outcomes at the front of your mind as you progress through the chapter. Some exercises ask you to think about something which generates negative feelings. Where this is the case, as in the first exercise, you can use one of your brilliant examples.

exercise 3.1   ## How you create your response to events

Part 1

1   Bring to mind someone you don't particularly like, or with whom you have very strong conflicting opinions.

2   As you think about this person pay attention to how they are appearing in your thoughts. Notice whether they are doing or saying anything.

3   Does the person appear in your mind as real life, in full colour, or is the image you have of them duller or brighter than real life in any way?

4   Do they appear as a large or small image?

5   Where is this image located? Is it projected in front of you, to one side, above or below eye level?

6   Do you hear a voice? Describe the tone of voice.

7   How are you feeling now after paying so much attention to these aspects of your thinking?

8   Have a shake-out and take a deep breath. Clear your mind in preparation for the next part of this exercise.

Part 2

Bring to mind someone you really like, and who you know likes you.

Go through the same procedure as above paying attention to each of the following aspects of your internal representation of this person:

●   size of the image

●   location of the image

●   amount of detail in the image

●   brightness and contrast of the image

●   whether lighter or darker than real life

●   any words or sounds, voice tone.

How are you feeling now after paying so much attention to these aspects of your thinking?

How to get the most from this exercise

Solo. Read through Part 1 of the exercise and commit it to memory. Then put the book down, relax and take yourself through the steps. Do the same for Part 2. Frequent reference to the written procedure will require you to keep shifting your focus and this will inhibit the exercise.

Duo. As a practitioner or coach guiding the explorer through the exercise, be sure to establish good rapport from the outset, and then give the explorer clear instructions. Notice how quickly the explorer is processing and keep to their pace. Some people process images very quickly, while others need more time to put their images together. Avoid using words like 'can you' and 'try' both of which offer the possibility of failure. By giving direct instructions, as described in the exercise, the explorer is better able to concentrate on doing the exercise.

Make sure you are not facing the explorer square on; position yourself slightly to one side so that you don't interfere with the explorer's ability to create mental images.

How does this exercise work?

When you have a negative experience, for example a strong argument with someone, your memory of the event will consist of still pictures or short movies, sounds and feelings. When you want to recall this experience you access this information by transferring the stored images, sounds and feelings from your memory banks into the forefront of your mind. As the pictures and sounds are revealed to you so the feelings take hold. The most fascinating aspect of this process is the precision with which these memories are recreated. Try it and notice this precision. The colours, size and location of images will be identical each time you access the same memory.

You are now programmed to feel a certain way when you think of the past event, so that when you next encounter the person or situation which featured in the event the very same feelings are recreated, and you respond accordingly.

At this stage you are merely exploring your mind and discovering how it has been working all these years. Shortly you will learn how to use this knowledge to make very quick and permanent changes to both your thinking process and how you feel.

brilliant presupposition

'I am in control of my mind and therefore my results.'

The more you take control of your own thought process, the more responsibility you take for your results and, therefore, the less you are likely to blame other people or external events for the situations in which you find yourself.

exercise 3.2   How to change your responses

This exercise builds on the awareness drawn from the previous exercise and introduces you to a very simple NLP technique to literally reprogramme the way you have already coded a past memory.

Use the same example you used in Exercise 3.1, Part 1, i.e. a person you dislike, or with whom you have very strong conflicting opinions. Alternatively, use your brilliant example.

Describe the following aspects of your mental representation:

- Size of the image?
- Physical location (exactly where does the image appear in your mind's eye – is it above eye level, down, to one side, or in front of you?)
- Distance projected – is it close to you, or away at some distance?
- Brightness level?
- Contrast?
- Colour or black and white?
- Are there any sounds with your image?

Now imagine adding whitewash to your image, and as you do notice the image getting paler and paler, then begin to push it away into the distance. Any sounds can be turned down so they become softer and harder to hear, with you eventually being unable to make out what the sound is as it is so faint. Watch the image move further and further away and get whiter and whiter, then become aware of how much better you are feeling.

Congratulate yourself for taking control!

How to get the most from this exercise

Solo. Read through the exercise and commit it to memory, and then put the book down, relax and do the exercise. If your image doesn't want to move, or if it resists the whitewash, imagine it being printed on a piece of flimsy film and watch it float away as a strong breeze carries it off over the horizon and out of sight.

Duo. Establish rapport and give the explorer clear instructions. You can make this exercise more effective by using hand gestures to emulate the image being sent off into the distance, or floating away. To do this put your palm in the location of the image and pull it back and up at the same time. This may seem a peculiar thing to do, but when done elegantly the explorer will respond.

If the explorer is associated with their image, that is they are in the image as if reliving it over again, have them step backwards out of it while you hold it still, and then have them whitewash it and send it away.

How does this exercise work?

If you have recalled a past negative memory repeatedly, your mind develops the habit of presenting the memory in a very specific way every time. It's as if you have no control over this process, but learning to control your mental images and sounds is just the same as learning to ride a bicycle. With persistence and practice you eventually succeed.

Before moving on, think about some specific scenarios where you want to have a positive impact such as making a phone call to a prospective client or employer, presenting to a group, selling a product or service, making a significant purchase, learning a new skill, exercising or training. As you think about doing one of these things, what kind of image pops into your mind? What feelings does the image create? Is this feeling setting you up for a successful or enjoyable experience? If not, you know what to do.

'You have all the resources you need to change.'

It may appear that a negative memory is something you are stuck with, but feeling stuck just means that you haven't yet learned what you need to release yourself and move on. However, the ability to learn how to do this is within you.

Representation systems

Engaging with the world around you involves all the senses of sight, sound, feeling, smell and taste, and the use of our senses varies greatly from person to person. Our senses access information and take it in so that we can process it and communicate something back out into the world. Some people use one sense to access information and another to process it. Each sense is a system, or channel of information access and processing, and the unique way each person uses their sensory systems creates their personalised 'map of the world'. The greater your awareness of the role sensory systems play in creating your unique map the more control you can have over your feelings. First awareness and then change.

Lead system

The lead system is the first to react to a stimulus; for example, if you ask me a question, as I listen to you I may create or recall an image in my mind which relates my experience with what you have asked. This might be followed quickly by how I feel about it, or I could hear sounds relating to the question. I used my visual system to make the initial connection with the topic of your question and then hand over to another sense to process the question and come up with a response.

Preferred system

This system is the one I prefer to use over the others to process infor-mation. I will use all the sensory systems in various combinations and sequences, and the one which dominates more than the others will be my preferred system. This is the system which the lead system hands over to.

One of the ways you can recognise another person's lead and preferred systems is by their eye accessing cues. The preferred system can also be recognised by the sensory words, or predicates the person is using, e.g. 'I **see** what you mean', 'It **feels** fine to me' or 'I **hear** what you say'. You will learn more about the use of predicates to build rapport in Chapter 6.

brilliant presupposition

'All behaviour is state dependent.'

Whatever you want to do, you can optimise your results by getting yourself into an appropriate state of mind/body before you begin. So the next time you attend a training course, make sure you arrive in an optimum state of curiosity and exploration so you can soak up the learning on offer. It doesn't make sense to arrive at a course with a mind/body state of cynicism or arrogance as these states tend to block the learning process, but some people do.

exercise 3.3   How to read eye-accessing cues

This exercise builds on the two previous exercises in this chapter by deepening your awareness of how you think, and showing how another person is thinking from the way they move their eyes. The eyes are windows into the mind, and you will use what you learn in the next exercise to enhance your personal change techniques and to have a positive influence on other people.

For this exercise you will need to work with another person. Prepare a series of questions or commands which ask for different sensory based information. For each of the following examples come up with two more of your own:

Visual

What do you **imagine** public transport will **look like** in 100 years from now?

Example 1:

_____

Example 2:

_____

Auditory

Describe the **sound** of a motorcycle engine revving.

Example 1:

_____

Example 2:

_____

Kinaesthetic

What does it **feel like** to have a hot shower at the end of a **tiring** day?

Example 1:

_____

Example 2:

_____

Internal dialogue (self-talk)

What do you **say to yourself** when you know you are going to be late for an important meeting?

Example 1:

_____

Example 2:

_____

Now position yourself so you can watch the other person's eye movements as they respond to your commands and questions. Some people like to project their mental images off into the distance, so sit at an angle rather than directly opposite so that you leave their field of projected vision clear.

Refer to the eye accessing cues diagram overleaf and note which type of thinking relates to each eye position. Familiarise yourself with this diagram before continuing.

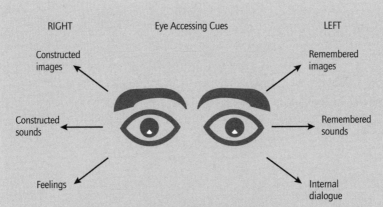

RIGHT   Eye Accessing Cues   LEFT

Constructed   Remembered
images   images

Constructed   Remembered
sounds   sounds

Feelings   Internal
                                                              dialogue

Note: this represents observing another person's accessing cues, i.e.
remembered images are up to their left, and is for a right-handed
person. A left-hander may have left switched with right.

Each of your eyes is connected to both sides of your brain, and so as you stimulate the part of your brain that processes images your eyes will move accordingly. The same goes for sounds, feelings and internal dialogue. It is a peculiar sensation to attempt to keep your eyes still while thinking and talking – it's one way to force your mind to slow down or almost grind to a halt.

Watch the eyes as you ask your question and notice whether they go up, down, left, right or just stare straight ahead. Some eye movements will be slow and others very fast like a flicker. You may also find the eyes moving in a sequence, for example, first up to the left, then across and to the right, followed by down to the right.

As you observe the other person's eyes moving, and after they have finished processing your command or answering your question, feed back what you noticed. Ask them if they were accessing images, sounds or feelings, or if they were talking to themselves. Check out if their eye movements correspond to their experience of responding to you.

How to get the most from this exercise

Solo. Don't even try it – you will go boggle-eyed looking in the mirror!

Duo. You may notice that the response does not always correspond with the eye accessing cue diagram. Even though you ask a visual type question your partner may respond by accessing auditory information, feelings or internal dialogue, or a mix of two or more. This may be because some channels are more frequently used and therefore better developed than the others. Don't expect your partner to match the diagram exactly – few people do in our experience, but you should find some consistency with it. Pay attention also to the lead and reference systems. If you ask an auditory question, for example, your partner may access an image initially in order to get to the sound. If your partner is left-handed, their accessing cues may be reversed left/right, but not necessarily. Some left-handers follow the right-handed configuration.

🏃 **brilliant** action

Spend some time observing people's eye movements and notice whether they are accessing visual, auditory or kinaesthetic channels when they are processing. See how many people you can catch with their eyes down talking to themselves. When you get used to this ask a question now and again like 'how are you seeing this', or 'what do you tell yourself about this' and notice the response when you get it right.

The physiology of VAK

In addition to eye accessing cues and sensory words, there are other indicators of *visual* (V), *auditory* (A) and *kinaesthetic* (K) preferences.

- **Visual indicators.** Because thinking is done in pictures the process is faster than the other channels A and K. So speech tends to be faster in order to keep up with the mental images flashing or streaming through the mind. This causes breathing to be from the chest and the voice to be pitched high.

- **Auditory indicators.** Sound is slower than imagery so there will be a more moderate pace to speech. Breathing is from the solar plexus and body language tends to be controlled with precision in movement.

- **Kinaesthetic indicators.** A slow process of feeling the way through a conversation, so speech is slower, breathing from the lower abdomen, and voice tone deeper. There may also be pauses in speech to check the feelings now and again.

When you combine all these various aspects of a person's representation system, and develop your sensory acuity to notice more, you can begin to respond in ways which really connect with other people at a deep level. This will be covered further in the chapter on rapport.

Sensory System	Eyes (for right-hander)	Words	Breathing	Voice
Visual	UP left recall right construct	See Picture Vision Imagine Look View	Upper chest area Fast pace	High pitched Fast pace
Auditory	LATERAL left recall right construct	Hear Talk Describe Explain Discuss Read Tune in	Solar plexus Even pace	Even pitch Medium pace
Kinaesthetic	DOWN (right)	Feel Grasp Shape Hold Smooth Gritty	Lower abdomen Slow pace	Low pitch Slow pace with pauses

Often the times when you sense communication is not working, or what is generally called a 'personality conflict' is just a mismatch between V, A and K systems. A person communicating in visual mode to someone processing kinaesthetically is likely to get out of sync and generate some frustration on both sides. You may have experienced this yourself with certain people. The more you notice, the more you can match and the easier communication becomes.

Now you have an awareness of how you use your sensory representation systems to think, and the indicators which reveal the specific V, A and K processes, you can use this information in various NLP exercises to change some of your negative representations, or those of a client or colleague.

 **presupposition**

'Mind and body are part of the same system.'

When you have a feeling in your stomach it is created by a thought. Thoughts precede feelings, and the thought affects the body through the central nervous system. Trying to act as if the mind and body are disconnected causes dissociation from life. You live life to the full by feeling it, and it begins in the mind with one solitary thought.

Collapsing negative feelings

An international tennis player developed a period of poorer than usual performance. He began to lose matches against less experienced players. When questioned, he explained this by saying he didn't like playing on grass and found hard courts more to his liking. Further probing revealed that in one particular match played on grass he had made a number of mistakes which caused him to lose badly to an unseeded opponent. Since that match whenever he had a game on grass the memory of the loss came flooding back and with it the feelings he had at the time. Over a season this stifled his performance and affected his ranking among international players. The next exercise collapsed the negative feelings attached to the original bad game and replaced them with the excitement he used to feel regardless of the surface he was playing on. His game recovered immediately and he went on to reclaim his international ranking.

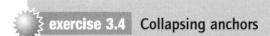

exercise 3.4   Collapsing anchors

For this exercise you will need a quiet place with about 3 metres of floor space.

1   On a sheet of paper draw an image surrounded by a blue square to represent the past situation to which you have anchored a negative feeling. Place this on the floor and stand on it as you recall the memory. Notice how you feel and where in the body you have this feeling.

2   Step away a metre to one side, take a deep breath and look up. Imagine the internal state or resource you would like to have the next time you are faced with this situation. Focus on inner resources such as confidence, patience, focus, determination, persistence, relaxation, courage, motivation, bring-it-on, humour, compassion, etc. Take your time to identify what it is you really would like to be like.

3   Move away from the original position another metre or so and place another piece of paper containing an orange circle on the floor. Stand on this as you bring to mind a time when you had the resource you identified in the previous step. Think of a situation where you were experiencing this resource state deeply. Notice the image which presents itself with this memory and crank up the colour, brightness and size. Turn up the volume and adjust the frequency range of any sounds to make it sound like full cinematic audio. If you are not already experiencing this memory as if you were truly reliving it then bring the image closer and step into it. Notice where your feelings are and send them moving around your entire body. As the feelings get stronger or deeper, and as they begin to peak, turn your head and glance at the original position where you placed the blue square.

4   How do you feel about the original situation now? If the exercise has worked, you may be laughing at yourself for reacting the way you did and recognising how ridiculous it all was.

5   Walk back to the original position and talk about the situation again. Try to have the negative feelings. If the exercise has worked well, you will not be able to bring back the negative feelings no matter how much you

try. They have been collapsed by the overpowering positive resource state you created.

How to get the most from this exercise

Solo. The blue square represents rules and restrictions with corners to get stuck in while the orange circle represents energetic growth, flow and abundance. This metaphor of shape and colour helps to generalise the experience across other similar situations and make the exercise more memorable. Make the shapes the same size and when you return to the original position pick up the orange circle and place it over your blue square.

Duo. Use the words THIS and THAT carefully in this exercise. When referring to the negative situation or blue square it is 'THAT situation or blue square'. When referring to the positive resource state or orange circle it is 'THIS resourcefulness or orange circle'. The words THIS and THAT imply distance and in this exercise you are working with emotional distance or association and dissociation. Using these words appropriately will enhance the impact of the exercise.

How does this exercise work?

When you have a negative experience your memory captures your feelings as well as the imagery and sound of the event. When you recall the memory the feelings you had at the time come flooding back with it. It may not be the memory of the event which does this; it could be that you hear the voice of someone who was at the event, or see a picture of something which reminds you of it, which bring back the original negative feelings.

In the past you have not been able to recall the event or anything linking the event without feeling the same way because the anchor works so rapidly. By fixing an event to a position on the floor you are putting just enough physical and emotional distance between you and the event to allow you to create positive feelings. When you then look back at the original event while feeling very positive you collapse the negative emotional association with the event.

NLP has many techniques which work with your internal representation to give you more control over your internal state and your feelings. Some techniques are used to change your response to past events like the collapsing anchors exercise you have just done. This next exercise works on future events giving you access to resources you may want before you even know you want them.

exercise 3.5 Anchoring a resourceful state

States can be either resourceful or unresourceful. The latter acts as a limitation on your capabilities and the former gives you access to your inner resources such as strength, confidence, persistence, etc. In this exercise you will learn how to create a positive and empowering resourceful state by setting an anchor to trigger the state whenever you want to have it.

1 First choose an anchor you will use to trigger the resourceful state. This will be used later when you want to trigger the state by firing your anchor, and it can be visual, auditory, or a physical gesture. For the purposes of this exercise choose a physical trigger such as pressing together the thumb and index finger of one hand, or pressing your thumb into the palm of the opposite hand.

brilliant tip

This is an ideal exercise to create and anchor the internal resources you identified as part of your well-formed outcome in Chapter 1.

2 Now decide what resource state you would like to anchor for future activities. Some people anchor confidence and fire it just before they give a presentation. Some people anchor patience or compassion to help them in situations where their tendency is to be confrontational. Any situation which creates anxiety as you think about it will give you a result with this exercise. I will refer to your resource state of choice as 'state x'.

3 Recall a time when you had a strong feeling of state x, and keep thinking about this memory. Notice the submodalities of your internal representation, the imagery, sounds and feelings. Take each modality in turn and intensify the internal representation. Turn up the colour, brightness, contrast and any sound. Make the image bigger and bring it closer until your feelings get stronger or deeper (strength for feelings such as confidence and courage, depth for feelings such as patience and compassion).

4 Focus on the feeling and spread it around your body, leading it up to your head, down your arms to the fingertips and down your legs to the

tips of your toes. Increase this feeling and before it reaches a peak set your physical anchor. Press gently at first and slowly increase the pressure as the feelings continue to strengthen or deepen. As your feelings reach a peak, release your anchor.

5 Relax and take a few deep breaths, and do the exercise three more times. Repetition makes the anchor work more effectively.

6 Do something else to take your mind away from the exercise and then test the effectiveness of your anchor by firing it in exactly the same way as you set it. Precision is key. Make sure you press in exactly the same place with the same amount of increasing pressure. If the exercise has worked, state x will come flooding back instantly.

You now have a resource you can access any time you need it.

How to get the most from this exercise

Solo. Make sure your anchor is set just before state x peaks and released just a moment after the peak. This will ensure you anchor a strong or deep state x rather than a mediocre state x. When you fire the anchor and the feeling returns intensify the imagery and sounds. After practising this a few times this will happen automatically.

Duo. Help the explorer to make the feelings stronger or deeper with your voice tone. If state x is confidence then your voice tone needs to sound confident. If state x is patience then your voice tone needs to have a patient tone.

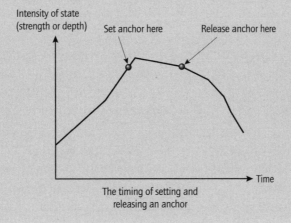

The timing of setting and releasing an anchor

How does this exercise work?

We all have certain stimulus-response behaviours programmed into our nervous system. The ring of the school bell, the colour of the traffic lights or smell of dinner being cooked all stimulate a response of some kind which becomes automatic after only a few occurrences. Every day we are responding automatically in a very precise way to what we see, hear, smell, taste and touch. Advertisers know this all too well and attempt to saturate our senses with mindless ditties and images that stick in our heads. They are hoping that when you think of buying a product their advertising will pop up in your mind first and strongest.

This exercise uses this natural tendency to respond with precision to a stimulus, but here you do it consciously and to anchor a response you really want. The following exercises are all designed to help you change unresourceful states into resourceful states using what you have learned about representation systems and states. You can either use your learning examples or choose something else you would like to change.

 exercise 3.6 **Swish technique**

This is one of the earliest NLP procedures and is highly effective at re-programming the way you think about something which causes anxiety, frustration, anger or sadness.

1　Recall a specific past interaction where you responded in a way that generates concern as you think about it now. It could be a meeting, a telephone call, conversation or a presentation – any interaction where you would like to change the way you think and feel about the event.

2　As you think about this event, notice the picture which comes into your mind. Check how you are feeling as you focus on this image. This next part might seem odd, but it is important. Increase the size of your image. Make it brighter and more colourful and bring it closer. This should make the feelings worse. Have a shake-out and clear your mind.

3   Decide what resources would help you deal with this situation effectively and then construct a new image of a time when you were using these resources effectively. Make sure that you include all the resources you need – confidence, clarity of thought, listening ability, creativity, questioning ability etc. Notice the image you have and check that this thought creates a strong feeling of resourcefulness. Push the image away, make it smaller and see the colour drain out until it becomes like a small grey postage stamp.

4   Bring back your first unresourceful image and place your second 'grey postage stamp' image in the bottom corner of your first image. The next step requires speed. As you say to yourself 'swish', instantaneously collapse the large picture while making the new self-image large and bright.

5   Repeat step four about five times, ensuring that you 'break state' between each one. Speed and repetition are essential.

6   To test your new 'response', trigger the state again by imagining a future time when you will want this different response. This is called 'future pacing'. Imagine the event that would trigger your state. If you still get the original response, go back to step one and do it again, although by the time you have swished your images five to six times you will find that the new state swishes itself. You will have a new, more resourceful way of responding to this interaction.

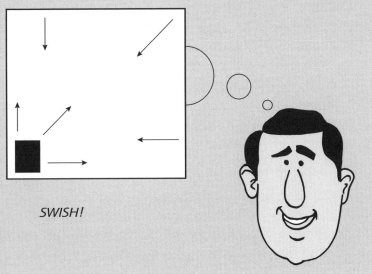

SWISH!

exercise 3.7   Submodality mapping

This exercise is useful where you have a particular way of thinking that limits your capability. It may not be such a worrying situation, but you may be frustrated at your lack of results in a certain area. It uses the submodalities of your visual representation to create fast and enduring change. Here are some examples for using this exercise:

- from poor decision-making to smart decision-making

- from lack of focus to laser focus

- from uncertainty to absolute certainty

- from impatient to patient

- from risk aversion to risk exploration.

Let's take decision-making as an example.

1   Bring to mind a time when you made a poor decision. Notice the colour qualities of the image, the location and size. Is it colour or black and white? Pay particular attention to the location and size of this image.

2   Take your time to think of a smart decision you took that went well. Notice the colour qualities of the image, the location and size. It will most likely be in a different location from your first image. Now compare the differences between the qualities of these two images., i.e. the difference in your thinking between a poor and a smart decision.

3   Choose something you are undecided about. Notice the image location, size and colour qualities. Take this image and move it into the location of your smart decision image. The content of the picture remains the same but turn the qualities into the qualities of the smart decision image.

4   While focusing on this image, in its new location, describe how you are going to come to a decision on the topic in hand.

How to get the most from this exercise

Submodalilities have a precision about them. Every time you think a particular way the imagery, sound and feelings will unfold in precisely the same configuration, i.e. your thought process. The more aware you are of the difference between an effective process and an ineffective one the closer you are to making a positive change. When you sense the same configuration occur you can map it on to a more effective thought process.

The key to this exercise is the precision in mapping across from one location to another.

Solo. This is easy enough to do on your own, just make sure you can recall the exact location of both images.

Duo. Sometimes the explorer may say the image won't move. Find creative ways to help the image map across. Having it float across works well, or sliding it across slowly. Maybe make it fade out and re-appear in the new location. Whatever works for the explorer.

 ### exercise 3.8 Spinning feelings

This exercise works particularly well for people who may not be creating clear mental pictures, and for those who tend to associate fully with their past memories, causing them to feel overwhelmed by emotion. It is effective for everyone else too.

1 Bring a past experience to mind over which you have been worrying in some way, and where you would like to be more resourceful. Notice the feelings you have as you focus on this past situation.

2 Notice where in your body you are feeling the emotions and which way the feeling is moving (feelings usually have a rotational movement).

3 Imagine the feeling leaving your body and visualise it some distance away between 2 and 6 feet in front of you. See it spinning. Slow down the spin until it stops and then spin it the opposite way. Give your feeling a positive symbolic image and spin it faster and faster.

4 Imagine bringing the feeling back inside you with it spinning in this new direction. Grow the feeling; send it spinning around your entire body from the tips of your fingers to the tips of your toes to the crown of your head. Enjoy the feeling as you bring back to mind the original thought which used to worry you, but now is nothing at all.

▶

How to get the most from this exercise

Take your time and really sense where your feelings are and how they are moving. When we talk about our feelings we are usually referring to our emotions, and emotions are always moving around. The word itself means 'move out'. When you can tune in to your feelings in this way, you can make some amazing changes by spinning them in the opposite direction.

Solo. This is easy enough to do on your own; just make sure you can stay with the process without any interruptions.

Duo. Help the explorer with your instructions by using a voice tone congruent with the desired state. Express the desired emotion with your voice and your gestures – it all helps to lead the explorer through the process.

CHAPTER 4

Empower yourself with positive beliefs

There's no future in this any more

Michael had been in sales for over 10 years and had been very successful. In the past six months, however, his results were below target, which he put down to a belief that his industry was in decline. His colleagues complained that it was becoming harder to meet targets and this negativity made him feel worse. One day he decided it was time to find a more lucrative product to sell. In his search he met Paula, a career coach and NLP master practitioner.

As Michael was telling Paula how he felt, she picked out a number of statements which she thought worthy of challenge.

- 'My clients are cutting back their budgets.'
- 'There's no future in this any more.'
- 'It's getting harder to make a sale.'

To the untrained ear these remarks are just statements describing Michael's experience, but to Paula they set alarm bells ringing as possible limiting beliefs. She asked him some questions to clarify and challenge these belief statements.

All your clients? Which ones are cutting back? Could there be other companies who are not cutting back, but are not yet clients of yours? No future at all? What if all the other sales executives moved to another industry, might this put you in a position to clean up? Is it really getting harder, or do you just need to be selling smarter? What if it was more about your sales skills? Could the competition be investing more in their sales skills? What evidence are you basing these beliefs on?

▶

When something becomes difficult it is all too easy to blame circumstances and give up. Then limiting beliefs become stronger and prevent creative thinking. Paula's questions caused Michael to re-examine the specific experiences which led to him forming his beliefs. He realised that he had been growing these beliefs from a very small amount of evidence. What if he was wrong? What if he had been writing off customers without really checking their commitment? How many assumptions and false perceptions had he been creating and then projecting on to prospects he hadn't yet approached? He re-evaluated his position and decided to give it another chance. He remembered the feeling from his early years in sales, as if possibility was limitless, and began to think creatively again.

Within the first two weeks of deciding to give it another go he pulled in a major sale from a client he had previously written off. From there he went on to win more sales each week. He stopped listening to the repetitive negative chatter of his colleagues, focused his attention on his selling skills and started cleaning up.

Beliefs can either hold you back or propel you forward, and they are usually based upon very little evidence. When we listen to other people's statements, we tend to accept what they tell us and then respond with our own experience, often giving solutions. It doesn't seem polite to challenge what people say, unless we have a vested interest in doing so. This means that your own statements, some of which could be limiting your potential, will remain unchallenged. So if you are going to carry around a bunch of beliefs about life, work and relationships, wouldn't you want them to be empowering, urging you towards success rather than limiting your potential?

 brilliant overview

You are about to learn:

● How to identify beliefs from everyday conversation

● How to test if a belief is limiting the potential to make progress

● How to challenge a limiting belief using a precision language model

● How to use outcomes to create the desire to change

● How to build new positive empowering beliefs.

brilliant examples

Think of something which causes you frustration, or an ambition you have set for yourself. Write your concerns, desires, fears, hopes or frustrations about this under the relevant categories below. Keep your comments brief. You will come back to them as you progress through this section of the workbook.

1   An aspect of your work.

_____

_____

_____

2   A relationship.

_____

_____

_____

3   Something else you feel you are struggling to achieve.

_____

_____

_____

 **action**

If you feel there is an obstacle to the pursuit of something important to you, listen to your words. Pay attention to your language and tone of voice and analyse your words, listening for self-imposed limitations such as 'I'm no good at x' or 'I'll never be able to x' or 'they wouldn't want to x'. Now seek the evidence to prove the statements untrue.

Words, experience and interpretation

Words flow quickly, so quickly that the meaning very often evades understanding. In many cases false assumptions are made. This is exacerbated when the medium for communication is electronic. Technology has brought many major benefits to society, enabling business to be more agile and people to become more entrepreneurial, but the tendency to cut down and speed up messages makes the electronic method of communication easy to abuse.

The words used to describe an experience are an abstraction of the experience itself. To fully describe everything you saw, heard and felt for an event that lasts a mere five minutes would make conversation unbearably dry and lengthy. Conversation is inevitably cut down and abstracted through three processes:

- **Generalisation** – the tendency to categorise similar experiences.
- **Deletion** – paying attention to some things and not others.
- **Distortion** – attaching meanings through evaluation and judgement.

Words are an interpretation of experience. It is this interpretation which contains the beliefs. In order to test the beliefs we can refer back to the factual experience. For example, in our story Michael's account of his predicament was described through belief statements such as 'it's getting harder to make a sale'. It is likely that he formed this belief from one or two experiences where existing clients had stopped buying from him. Paula invited Michael to review these specific experiences. In doing so he was encouraged to open up possibilities rather than close down all prospects through the belief that selling is getting harder.

Before delving into beliefs it is worth exploring some of the common barriers to good communication generally, since the language techniques you are about to learn require an ability to listen attentively to abstractions.

exercise 4.1   Barriers to effective listening

Here are four common ways that people prevent themselves from listening.

1 Having thoughts of higher status or knowledge

Being preoccupied with thoughts of self-importance will cause you to listen with a contaminated ear.

- I'm too busy/important to listen to this.
- This is of no use to me.
- This is below me.

Recall a time when you realised you hadn't been listening because you didn't think it was important enough to do so. Make a note here of the consequences of not listening on this occasion.

_____

_____

_____

2 Mental rehearsal of your own script

Being preoccupied with your own personal agenda. Construct your response when you have finished listening – not while the other person is talking.

Recall a time when you realised that you hadn't been listening because you were mentally rehearsing your response. Make a note here of the consequences of not listening on this occasion.

_____

_____

_____

3 Fixed opinion (judgement)

You have a fixed opinion about the situation or the speaker and you are making a judgement as the other person is speaking.

Recall a time when you realised that you hadn't been listening because you were judging. Make a note here of the consequences of not listening on this occasion.

_____

_____

_____

4 Disinterest (why am I here anyway?)

You don't have a strong purpose for listening and your mind will wander on to other things as the other person is speaking.

Recall a time when you realised that you hadn't been listening because you were disinterested. Make a note here of the consequences of not listening on this occasion.

_____

_____

_____

If you have a clear purpose and outcome for a communication, and one of the above barriers is preventing you from listening effectively, you are unlikely to engage the other person, or give them the impression that you understand them. When there is no understanding and no engagement, communication becomes very ineffective and the other person will resist your attempt to influence them. By learning to listen attentively and self-lessly you will hear the limiting beliefs and be able to challenge them with integrity and empathy. One of the key skills to master in NLP is sensory acuity – the ability to recognise changes in other people from your sensory input. This skill will be explored in further depth later in the book. If you are not listening attentively, you are likely to miss both auditory and visual information about the other person which may be useful to you.

brilliant presupposition

'Whatever you believe, it's true for you.'

Beliefs are generalisations – they are best guesses for things which have insufficient evidence for us to really know. The generalisation is also likely to have elements of deletion and distortion. It doesn't help to judge a belief as good or bad but whether it is useful, and because beliefs guide our behaviour it makes sense to hold beliefs that work for our better good rather than limit our potential.

How to identify beliefs from everyday conversation

A belief will be some form of statement about self, something or other people which is relatively easy to spot in conversation. Listen to any political debate and you will hear many beliefs in the form of opinions or judgements. Once we judge a politician to be a certain type of person we believe this to be true and expect him or her to behave accordingly. Beliefs are generalisations about something which we have formed a meaning about and they require very little evidence.

If I say that last week the bus was late twice, I might decide that the bus service is unreliable. That the bus was late twice last week may be true, but to extend this to the entire bus service being unreliable is a belief.

If I say that I was frustrated at writing a letter because I am useless at writing, being frustrated is possibly true, but being useless at writing is a belief.

If I damage my knee and my doctor tells me I will always have a problem with it, the damage to my knee is a fact but my doctor's prediction is a belief.

If my boss tells me to keep an eye on Mike because he's lazy, I might believe him and get on to Mike's case. My boss talking to me is a fact, but his reference to Mike being lazy is a belief, and one I might readily adopt.

If we accept our beliefs as true, then we become stuck with the belief. We stop looking for a solution or alternative possibility and accept the predicament we find ourselves in. Beliefs are very powerful and great care should be taken to ensure we avoid holding beliefs which limit us.

↗ **brilliant** presupposition

'The words are not the experience they represent.'

We may believe our own words and the words of others, but when we extend
our belief to the experience the words are relating to we do not know what that
experience really is. Be careful what you accept as belief from mere words alone.

Whatever you believe, it will be true for you. It may not be true for
another person. If a belief is stopping us from making a positive change,
maybe in a relationship, then we just tend to live with it. We also defend
our beliefs and protect them from attack by other people. It may sound
crazy, but some people will defend their right to believe that the world is
stacked against them.

We are also likely to seek further evidence to confirm a belief to be true,
and make excuses for the limitation rather than seek ways to overcome
it. But there is a positive side to this. Because beliefs are generalisations,
and are nothing more than a way of thinking, we can easily change them
should we wish to do so. A belief is not tangible; it has no substance. It
is a set of thoughts only, and NLP is very effective at changing the way
we think.

brilliant tip

If someone tells you that another person is unreliable, untrustworthy, lazy or
any other undignified trait, be careful about accepting wholeheartedly what
they tell you. Have part of you look for the opposite trait and form your own
conclusions.

How to test if a belief is limiting potential

Human beings are creative problem solvers. It is in our nature to seek new
and better ways of dealing with the challenges we face every day. This is
how we have evolved. It is natural to learn new skills and explore different

solutions, but sometimes we can become overwhelmed by choice, or over-anxious about a future event. We can feel guilt, regret and anger at past events. We can be obsessive, irrational and turn judgement in on ourselves to become a 24/7 victim of circumstances. We can let fear and frustration take control of our logic, and we can become desperate, lonely and depressed.

A limiting belief may be charged with a negative emotion which you will hear in the tone of voice and notice in the physiology – perhaps the breathing rate will change. If it is one which has been held for some time there may no longer be a visible display of emotion, but the construct of the statement will imply a state of being stuck in some way. In the examples which follow you will learn to recognise the many ways language can present a limiting belief statement.

How to challenge a limiting belief using a precision language model

The NLP meta model's categories provide a useful way of recognising limiting generalisations, deletions and distortions and then questioning their validity. Think of it as a toolkit for getting precision and clarity around limitations in such a way that it can shake a belief at its roots and open up the possibility for a new and more empowering belief.

exercise 4.2   Metamodel

Each category is presented with an example and a number of questions to gain clarity and precision. This first example is followed by a second to give you some practice in asking clarifying questions.

Categories

1 MODAL OPERATOR of POSSIBILITY – a statement which closes down possibility

Example 1: 'You *can't* build a business without making personal sacrifices.'

▶

Use questions which encourage the opening up of possibility, such as:

- What if you could?
- What sacrifices are you referring to exactly?
- What do you mean by build?

Come up with some questions for example 2.

Example 2: 'He's *not capable* of doing that job.'

- Q: _____
- Q: _____
- Q: _____
- Q: _____

2 MODAL OPERATOR of NECESSITY – a statement which closes down options and choice

Example 1: 'Children *need* discipline.'

Use questions which challenge the need, explore the origin of the statement and create alternatives, such as:

- What might happen if they didn't have discipline?
- All children?
- Is this all they need?
- What kind of discipline do you think they need?
- From whom?

Example 2: 'You *have to* follow the procedure.'

- Q: _____
- Q: _____
- Q: _____
- Q: _____

3 UNIVERSAL QUANTIFIER – *a statement which states that something is true for everything or everybody*

Example 1: *'Nobody loves me.'*

Use questions which suggest that the statement is ridiculous, or go along with it until the absurdity is apparent, such as:

- No one at all?
- Is there one person who might?
- How would/do people show their love for you?
- Do you love anyone?
- You mean that every person on this planet could never love you?

Example 2: 'My manager never listens.'

- Q: _____
- Q: _____
- Q: _____
- Q: _____

4 NOMINALISATIONS – *turning a verb or adjective into a noun and as a consequence deleting the action*

Example 1: 'I have concerns over his *performance.'*

*(the word **performance** is a nominalisation of **performing**)*

Use questions which ask for specific actions, such as:

- What concerns specifically?
- How did you arrive at your concerns?
- Are you concerned about all his performance, or just some?

Example 2: 'Financial independence is the key to success.'

- Q: _____
- Q: _____
- Q: _____
- Q: _____

▶

5 LACK OF COMPARISON – *a statement of scale which lacks a comparison*

Example 1: 'Her children are not *very bright*.'

Use questions which ask for the comparison, such as:

- Not bright compared with whom?
- Not bright in what way exactly?
- How bright do you think they should be?

Example 2: 'There's not enough focus on key targets.'

- Q: _____
- Q: _____
- Q: _____
- Q: _____

6 UNSPECIFIED VERB – *a verb which does not specify exactly 'how'*

Example 1: 'She *rejected* me.'

Use questions which request detail about the verb, such as:

- What did she do that you are calling rejection?
- Rejected in what way?
- So, you are feeling rejected? How did this happen exactly?

Example 2: 'We *messed up* the last project, didn't we?'

- Q: _____
- Q: _____
- Q: _____
- Q: _____

7 UNSPECIFIED REFERENTIAL INDEX – *pronouns such as those, them, it, we, etc.*

Example 1: '*They* were left to fend for themselves.'

Use questions which ask to specify the identity of a person, group or object.

- Who are they?
- All of them?

Example 2: *'There's* no focus on the budget.'

- Q: _____
- Q: _____
- Q: _____
- Q: _____

8 COMPLEX EQUIVALENCE – a statement in the form of 'X means Y'

Example 1: 'I know he doesn't love me because he never buys me flowers.'

Use questions to explore the logic in the relationship between X and Y:

- In what way does this mean that?
- What else could it mean?
- Does he show love any other way?

Example 2: 'Since they didn't give us the business we can't be a valued supplier.'

- Q: _____
- Q: _____
- Q: _____
- Q: _____

Example 3: 'I won't get the promotion; the boss doesn't even notice me.'

- Q: _____
- Q: _____
- Q: _____
- Q: _____

▶

9 CAUSE/EFFECT – a statement which states one thing caused another (A caused B)

Example 1: 'My children are driving me crazy.'

Use questions which expand on the relationship between cause and effect.

(In what way does this cause that?)

- What do your children do which causes you to go crazy?
- How is your craziness linked to your children?
- Does anyone or anything else cause you to go crazy, or is it just your children?

Example 2: 'He makes me mad.'

- Q: _____
- Q: _____
- Q: _____
- Q: _____

10 MIND READING – a statement which suggests the speaker knows what you are thinking

Example 1: '*I know* you don't want to support this initiative.'

Use questions which enquire 'how do you know that?'

- How do you know?
- You know what I'm thinking? How did you do that?
- You can read minds/my mind?

Example 2: '*Jim thinks* we're not up to the job.'

- Q: _____
- Q: _____
- Q: _____
- Q: _____

11 LOST PERFORMATIVE – a statement of fact or value judgement which excludes the source

Example 1: 'Standards in our industry are paramount.'

Use questions that request the source or origin of the statement.

- Who said that?
- Who are you quoting?
- What source are you quoting from?

Example 2: 'It's important to maintain our growth.'

- Q: _____
- Q: _____
- Q: _____
- Q: _____

How to get the most from this exercise

Solo. Read through each of the examples given and then go back and do the second example. Straight afterwards join in a conversation or switch on the radio or TV to a discussion or debate. Listen for the various categories and the beliefs which come flooding from the speakers' lips. Notice how in conversation it is common for a listener to accept the words as an accurate representation of the experience they represent. Imagine that you are in the discussion and fire off questions for practice.

Duo. As a practitioner or coach, it is useful to teach people to question their own language; to listen for the generalisations, deletions and distortions that may indicate a limitation for them. You can just question them, but once a person learns how to metamodel their own language, they can make their own belief changes.

You will now have a heightened awareness of limiting beliefs and be able to identify and challenge them in everyday language. There is a health warning which goes with the metamodel to save you from losing all your friends, and it's this, 'only ask a question when you have a clear purpose and outcome for doing so'. Remember that someone else's belief is important to them, even if it's holding them back. Even sceptics have a right to believe what they do, so it is a good idea to keep a healthy respect for their beliefs, even when testing and challenging their validity.

Now read through your statements at the beginning of this chapter and apply the metamodel to your own beliefs. Are they still valid? Were they ever valid? Could they be more empowering and supportive of your ambitions?

A belief is grounded in some personal experience and every belief will have its own set of submodality distinctions. A major difference will be noticed between beliefs which relate to possibility and beliefs which relate to limitation. Whatever the belief, before it can be broken it needs to be shaken, in order to open up the possibility that it might not be true. The following exercise uses submodality shifting to change a belief. Remember that you are free to experiment with your own beliefs, and to show sincere respect to others whose beliefs you may wish to change.

exercise 4.3   Fast belief change (using submodality mapping)

Part 1 Shaking the belief

1   Identify a limiting belief. As you think about this belief, notice the qualities of the image, particularly its position, size and colour.

2   Think of a belief you once had but that is now no longer true for you (Father Christmas or the Tooth Fairy tend to work well). As you think about this belief, notice the qualities of the image, particularly its position, size and colour.

3   Shift the submodalities of the limiting belief from step 1 on to the exact submodalities of the 'no longer true' belief in step 2, so that the location, distance, size, colour, brightness and contrast of your step 1 image become the same as the image in step 2.

Part 2 Exercising choice

1 Think of a more positive belief that you want to have instead of the limiting one. As you think about this belief, notice the qualities of the image, particularly its position, size and colour.

2 Identify a universal belief that you know to be absolutely true (the seasons change, for example). As you think about this belief, notice the qualities of the image, particularly its position, size and colour.

3 Shift the submodalities of the positive belief from step 1 on to the exact submodalities of the universal belief in step 2, so that the location, distance, size, colour, brightness and contrast of your step 1 image become the same as the image in step 2.

4 Try to think of the original limiting belief you started with. Do you feel different about it? Can you smile at yourself for having had that belief in the past? How does it feel having this new positively empowering belief?

How to get the most out of this exercise

Solo. Read the exercise and commit it to memory. This exercise is most effective when you are able to keep focused from beginning to end without breaking to read the next instruction.

Duo. As a practitioner or coach be sensitive to the speed at which the explorer is processing the images. You may need to speed up or slow down your instructions accordingly.

One of the popular applications of NLP is the cure of phobias, or irrational fears. When the thought of a future event or situation strikes you with panic and anxiety it is very inhibiting. Whether the phobia is a fear of spiders, lifts, public speaking, motorways, bridges, enclosed spaces, flying, dentists, or anything which creates a phobic response as it comes to mind, it can be cured simply with the Phobia Fix technique.

exercise 4.4   Phobia fix

1   Imagine that you are sitting in a film theatre and up on the screen you can see a black and white still picture in which you see yourself just before you had the phobic response.

2   Float out of your body up to the projection booth where you can watch yourself watching yourself – from here you see yourself sitting in the theatre watching the still picture up on the screen.

3   Now turn the snapshot on the screen into a black and white movie and watch it until just after the unpleasant phobic experience. When you get to the end, stop it as a slide. Then jump inside the picture and run it backwards in colour, adding cartoon music. Everything in the film will happen in reverse – people walking backwards and talking gibberish.

Now think about what it was you were being phobic about – see what you would see if you were actually there. Does it seem less of an issue? Do you feel relieved and free from the phobic chains?

How to get the most out of this exercise

You can tell a phobia from other types of worries and concerns by the physical change to the body and breathing when the person thinks about the phobia or concern. The exercise works by putting two levels of dissociation between the explorer and the thoughts which have been creating the phobic response. So you are looking at yourself looking at yourself on the cinema screen. From this dissociated viewpoint the explorer remains in control and is able to rationalise the situation while feeling calm about it. The visualisation will change the submodalities of the original thoughts responsible for the phobic response.

Solo. Read the exercise and commit it to memory, as this exercise requires concentration from beginning to end without breaking to read the next instruction. It is best to get someone to lead you through it.

Duo. As a practitioner or coach all you need to do is guide the explorer through the exercise, giving clear and direct instructions. This exercise is very easy and usually works first time. Help a nervous explorer by creating a kinaesthetic safety anchor which may be held throughout or used as required. To do this, just hold the person's arm and say 'OK, so we're both grounded here in the room together'. Should the explorer experience the phobic response at any time during the exercise, then apply the anchor you set at the beginning. Make sure you repeat it exactly; hold the arm in the same place with the same amount of pressure, and use the same voice tone when you speak.

CHAPTER 5

Driven by values

Educating Frances

Melvin: 'Frances, when are we going to start a family?'

Frances: 'As soon as I have finished my MBA.'

Melvin: 'You said that last year when you were completing your
Law degree.'

Frances: 'I promise this time, only two more years to go.'

Melvin: 'And in the meantime you are getting so stressed.'

Frances was 30 years of age, a HR manager in a commercial bank.
She knew the importance of education but her partner was growing
increasingly concerned over her health. She agreed to employ a coach
who quickly pointed out that the pressure she was putting herself under
was causing the stress. This was no revelation, but what did surprise
Frances was the root of her behaviour.

Frances's father grew up in a poor family and was not given the
opportunity of a university education. He vowed that, whatever it
would take, his children would get the best education available. This
value on education was instilled in his children all through their
formative years and into adulthood. Because of this Frances continued
to gain qualifications whether she needed them or not. She really
wanted children, but this clashed with her thirst for qualifications. She
eventually stopped studying, her health improved immediately and the
couple had their first child within a year of making this decision.

The change Frances made with the help of a coach may seem obvious

▶

to you and me, but when you are the one with the value you do not always link your behaviour and any negative consequences to it. Since the behaviour becomes habitual, to the owner it is part of their character, and it can take a little digging to uncover values which have been inherited from a parent.

brilliant overview

You are about to learn:

- How your behaviour is linked to your values
- How to elicit a person's hierarchy of values
- The connection between values and beliefs
- How values affect your capability
- How values can be used to realign your behaviour with a clear purpose
- How to change a value which is creating negative consequences.

brilliant examples

Values drive you to do or not do certain things consistently and they provide criteria by which to measure yourself. Some people also judge others by their own values and use this to decide who their friends and employers will be. If you think there may be a value attached to the personal examples you came up with in the previous chapter, you can use this value with the exercises which follow. Alternatively, the first exercise will help you to elicit your hierarchy of values and you may prefer to take this approach.

Write the value/s you would like to explore here.

_____

_____

_____

_____

_____

How behaviour is linked to values

Values are extremely powerful filters in that they determine what you focus on and off, and what you tune in to and out of. In the story, Frances had been focusing on her education while ignoring her health and her desire to have children. Whenever these matters came up, she would find ways of tuning out so that she could concentrate on her work and her studies. There are only so many hours in the day, and your values will play a major role in directing your focus and your energy. All too often you find people are driven by something inside which they hold as highly important while on the outside you see stress and unhappiness.

Values also drive decision-making, providing a criterion by which to evaluate a decision as right/wrong or good/bad. Whatever we call a right or good decision will match one or more of our personal values. We will also judge other people by our own values, and this is where a great deal of conflict occurs. If we have a high value around punctuality and someone is frequently late, we may judge them as uncaring, disinterested and lazy. Of course, our judgements are quite often totally wrong, but we like to have answers to behaviour which violates our values.

Working with values often brings a major shift in behaviour. It can sometimes be that a new value is adopted, but often personal change happens as a result of dropping a value which has not been working well, perhaps causing stress, conflict or distracting from other important endeavours.

You may notice a similarity between values and metaprogrammes which were covered in Chapter 2. The main difference is that personal values are ideas we hold about what is important in the world, and they drive a range of different behaviour which may change as soon as the value is dropped. A metaprogramme describes a consistent pattern of behaviour within a life context, such as work, family or a social circle.

The key questions to ask when linking behaviour to values are 'do my values work positively for me, and am I happy doing what I consider to be important?'

exercise 5.1   Values elicitation

This exercise will help you to create awareness around your values relating to a specific area of your life and thus discover what is really important and driving you. Choose either work, relationships or some other area of your life which you may feel isn't working for you as well as you would like. The exercise will refer to your chosen area as X.

Part 1

Ask the question, 'what is important to you about X?'

Keep asking the same question, 'what else is important to you about X?'

Write each answer on a separate white card.

Keep asking the question until you are sure you have elicited all the values. Sometimes the most obvious pop out last, so be patient and take plenty of time to think.

For example, if X is your work, you would ask 'what is important about your work? The answers could be 'the team/doing a good job/making a difference/achieving goals/learning/variety/accomplishments/having difficult challenges/coaching others'. Each one of these would be written on a white card.

Part 2

Create a hierarchy by comparing one value with the next and asking:

Which is the more important of these two values?

Continue until you have elicited at least the top three values. If you get 'stuck' at any time you can recap by asking:

If you had (repeat back the values), what else would be important to you about your work?

For example, take the first two values and ask, 'which is more important to you about your work, the team or doing a good job?' Let's say the answer is 'doing a good job', the next question is, 'which is more important to you about your work, doing a good job or making a difference?' Continue through all the other values in the same way.

Part 3

Take the top three values one by one and ask the question:

What does this value get for you?

List your answers and notice if anything seems to have too high or too low a value attached.

For example, if the top value is 'making a difference'. The answer to the question 'what does this value get for you?' might be, 'a feeling of satisfaction, of having had a positive impact'.

How to get the most out of this exercise

The aim of this exercise is to bring your values into the front of your mind in a systematic way so that you can check their current validity and make a change should you wish to do so. The outcome may be that you are happy with your values and don't want to make a change, or you may wish to change one or more values, in which case the process will have already begun. In most cases the revelation alone that a value is no longer wanted is enough to create a desired change.

Solo. You will need to be focused, disciplined and relaxed to do this exercise on your own. It may seem a little tedious to keep asking yourself the same question, but persistence and patience will reap rewards. Keep going through the process and notice what images, sounds, words and feelings arise. What are these signals suggesting?

Duo. Your sensory acuity is required here. You are not just taking the other person through a procedure; you are watching and listening for their responses, giving them time to process information and checking if they are 100% sure about their selections. If they indicate uncertainty, work with them to explore this. Be careful not to offer them your opinions; allow them to process for themselves.

Some people know their values very well; others get a little mixed up about what is really important and what really isn't important. Mix-ups can happen for a number of reasons, and they can be easily overlooked by being too busy to question whether what you are doing is valuable or not. Sometimes you can ask the question, and feel that something you are doing is not so

▶

important, but then carry on just the same because of habit. The last exercise may seem simple and repetitive, and yet this is what makes it so powerful. All you need to do to check the value you are putting on the various things you do is to take an hour or so out of your busy schedule and ask a friend to take you through the exercise. What comes up for you as you go through it may well surprise you, and could lead to a significant change of activity, work or even lifestyle.

Mixed-up values

There are some common causes for values becoming mixed up. You may recognise mixed-up values by feeling that something just isn't as it should be which may cause you to question why you do certain things. You may be able to come up with rational answers, but the discomfort remains. Anything can be justified if it suits.

Inherited values

As in Frances's story at the beginning of this chapter, inherited values come from one or both of your parents. You often find that parents' values tend to get drummed into their children. Maybe you were sent to dance classes or music lessons regularly and as you grew up you created a life around dance or music. Some children are given strict regimes of study and they grow to become studious as an adult. Because your behaviour is a big part of your identity you put a high value on the inheritance and continue to do it. This can work well for some people and not so well for others. In Frances's case, her value on studying was useful up to a point, to help her secure a career, after which it became a burden. Parents often want to give their children something they never had, and sometimes people decide to have children just so they can redress the balance and compensate for their own childhood deprivation. For some children this compensation can become a burden.

Rebellious values

There seems neither rhyme nor reason as to why one sibling might inherit a parental value and another rebel against it, but it happens. Wondering why this is the case may not help us deal with any negative consequences. Rebellion may spur a child on to greater things in adult life, to fight for a cause or uphold human values like justice, equality and respect or it can lead to criminal activity.

It is more useful to ask 'what' happened, and focus on a solution than ask 'why' and focus on the reasons. NLP is effective as a change technology because of this – looking for practical solutions and not getting tied up in academic theory where there is little evidence to determine an absolute answer for everything. We emphasise this point here because values are usually where people ask 'why' because they want to understand why a person does something. If you want a solution it is more effective to ask 'what' and 'how' questions.

Adopted values

At times we may find ourselves in an unfamiliar situation, like working for a new company, marrying into a family with different values from your own, or coping with an ailing parent or grandparent. Integration with the new group, or coping with the new situation can be achieved by adopting values from others in the same group. This value adoption drives a commitment to achieve something as long as the unfamiliar situation lasts. When your situation changes you may drop the value, or change it for something different.

Cultural values

These are possibly the strongest values of all. International companies are still seeking ways of bringing teams together from different countries to work under a common set of values such as timing, agreement, decision-making and trust. Whilst there are always exceptions to the general view of cultural nuances, when you visit another country it is these nuances that tend to stand out. For example, project leaders in a commercial bank in London became increasingly frustrated with their outsourced Indian partners because of the delay in authorising decisions through their strict hierarchy. They had failed to account for the cultural differences in decision-making when setting up the outsourcing agreements. When business plans go off-track because of these differences it often causes frustration and mistrust.

 action

Go back to your list of values from the earlier exercise and identify any which might fit into the categories: inherited, rebellious, adopted and cultural values. Are they still serving you well? Have any of them outlived their usefulness?

Values and beliefs

To be successful in any endeavour requires a wholehearted commitment to making things work, especially when you experience difficult times. A company that loses the commitment of its employees is likely to be beaten by the competition. When you are less than 100% committed to any endeavour you flag and become distracted when things get tough. This is where values come in. The more committed you are to something the higher value you put on it, not monetary value, but personal value. This high value then transforms into energy and drive to see things through.

Values are supported by beliefs; for example, a value for being honest will create beliefs about honesty and dishonesty. You may believe that someone who tells even a little white lie is a dishonest person and you might treat them as such. You would use honesty as a criterion for choosing friends and for judging work colleagues and your experience of doing so will form beliefs about who is and who isn't an honest person. Your own behaviour will also be self-scrutinised for honesty.

The tree of values and beliefs

You can think of a value as the trunk of a tree and the core beliefs which attach to the value as the roots feeding the belief, and the fruit is the growth of even more beliefs which all spring from the value. Whether a value or a belief comes first usually depends upon the experience, but this question is not as important as whether either is useful to you in some practical way. Take Simon as an example. He wanted to be the top sales-person in his company. Being number one had been a theme in his life; even as a child he was extremely competitive. He was driven by a number of core beliefs, namely:

- Being number 2 isn't good enough.
- People only recognise number 1.
- You have to stay on top to be really successful.

These core beliefs are the roots attached to the trunk value of 'Being number 1 is important'. Over time he had also accumulated more specific beliefs from his experience, namely:

- I can beat the others if I put the effort in.
- Mark and Lisa are lazy, I will easily beat them.
- Rick is smart and I will have to keep a close eye on him in case he cheats the system.
- The paperwork is slowing me down.
- I didn't reach number 1 last quarter because the system was unfair.
- My boss is making things difficult for me.

These beliefs are more like the fruit of the tree. They serve to surround the value in perceptions which strengthen the value over time. In Simon's case he started to create beliefs as excuses for not reaching number 1. When a belief is used in this way it is time to question the value itself, although many people find it too big a step to drop a value they have been holding for a long time. It often seems easier to build a bank of beliefs to excuse your shortfalls.

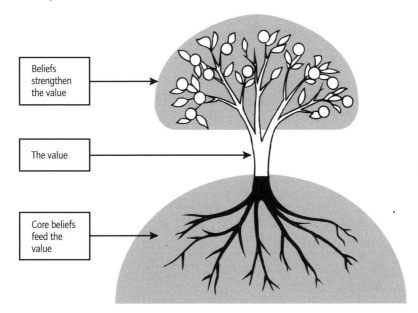

exercise 5.2   **Tree of value and beliefs**

Refer to the last exercise and choose one value to explore. It could be one that you feel may not be serving you well or may have outlived its usefulness.

Value (X):

_____

Now, think back to the very first time you recall having this value. Do you remember how it became so important to you? As you relive this memory write down any core beliefs which supported the value at that time, and which are still relevant to you today.

Core belief:

_____

Core belief:

_____

Core belief:

_____

Now think about a recent time where this value seemed really important to an actual experience. As you revisit this experience, make a note of any other beliefs that are connected specifically with this particular experience.

Specific belief:

_____

Specific belief:

_____

Specific belief:

_____

Specific belief:

_____

How to get the most from this exercise

Solo. Be open and honest with yourself. Search for beliefs that you may have used, and be using as an excuse to justify your value in some way. Is it really helping you?

Duo. Help the person by asking questions such as:

● What did you believe about this person/situation at the time?

● Is that belief still valid today?

● What else did you believe?

You can also use the questions in Chapter 3 on beliefs to check out the validity of a belief.

Alignment

When you attach a high value to something, the beliefs you connect with it have an impact on your capability and your behaviour. The diagram overleaf shows where values and beliefs fit into the overall process of aligning behaviour. This alignment model, as it is commonly referred to, shows the impact various neurological levels have over one another.

The term 'neurological' refers to your nervous system which is what all your senses feed into. So when you see, hear, smell, taste and feel, the information taken in is carried by your central nervous system. Your behaviour is influenced by a combination of different levels of thinking which result from the way your central nervous system responds to the outside world. One person may react in a stressful way to the smell of a hospital whilst another might respond in a more relaxed way. It all depends on how the person has coded their experience of hospitals on their central nervous system through each of their senses.

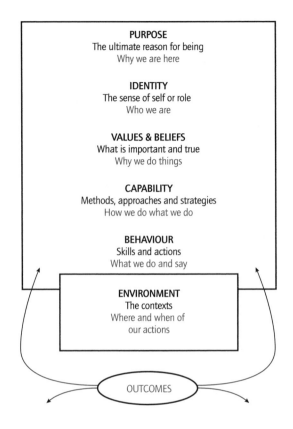

PURPOSE
The ultimate reason for being
Why we are here

IDENTITY
The sense of self or role
Who we are

VALUES & BELIEFS
What is important and true
Why we do things

CAPABILITY
Methods, approaches and strategies
How we do what we do

BEHAVIOUR
Skills and actions
What we do and say

ENVIRONMENT
The contexts
Where and when of
our actions

OUTCOMES

brilliant presupposition

'The mind and body are part of the same (central nervous) system.'

To think that we can be perfectly aligned as this model suggests is unrealistic. It is more likely that we make adjustments as we go through life, sometimes small ones and sometimes big ones, whenever we feel things are going in the wrong direction. There is rarely a point of alignment or equilibrium that is constant; everything everywhere is in a constant state of change, and so it seems to make more sense that we are constantly adjusting as we experience new things. So perfection isn't the goal, rather to have it in our nature to know when we are out of alignment and then know how to make a positive adjustment. This is where the tools of NLP come in; they provide an increased awareness and plenty of tools for change. It is the practising of these tools that develops the skill to create change.

A misalignment between levels can cause stress and frustration, distraction, variations in energy and in some extreme cases physical and mental illness. The model itself is the culmination of research by the anthropologist Gregory Bateson and insights from one of the early NLP developers, Robert Dilts. It is useful in determining at which level to make an intervention where your outcome is to positively influence learning, communication or change. In general terms, the level at which you make a change will definitely impact all the levels below, and may or may not influence the levels above.

The model has universal application. It can be used with personal change, with teams, an entire organisation or even culture. Consider Stephanie who works with a retail company in customer services. Her job is to send letters to customers who have complained about their products. She had been considered for promotion to head of her department but she turned it down on the basis that she didn't think her English was good enough and worried that the job might be too difficult for her.

When we questioned Stephanie it turned out that one of her teachers at school, over eight years ago, told her she ought to pursue a career in mathematics because her English was not very good. She took a job in accounting which she held for two years and disliked immensely. We read some of the letters she had written and they were extremely well composed. There was no real evidence that she was poor at English; in fact, there was plenty of evidence to the contrary. When you relate this example to the alignment model you see that the **belief** she accepted from her teacher, and the low **value** she adopted about her English ability acted as a limitation on her **capability** so that she restricted her **behaviour** to that of customer services coordinator, and this in turn affected her working **environment**. We asked her to find out from the current manager what being head of department would involve and were delighted to hear some weeks later that she had put herself forward for the job.

When you make a shift in alignment like Stephanie, you will find that things change and new outcomes are suddenly within your reach. These outcomes feed back into your capability and encourage further possibilities for change.

exercise 5.3   Alignment

This exercise is useful for checking your alignment to a specific outcome. Choose one of the outcomes you have already identified earlier in the book, or any outcome that is important to you now. If you are unsure about defining an outcome, revisit Chapter 1.

What outcome do you want to achieve?

_____

Define your higher purpose for wanting this outcome

_____

Define your role in pursuing this outcome

_____

Describe the values that are important to you about this outcome

_____

Describe what you believe about achieving this outcome ...

What do you believe about yourself, and your capability?

_____

What do you believe about others involved in your outcome?

_____

What do you believe about your chance of success?

_____

What makes you capable of achieving this outcome?

How are you going to achieve this?

_____

How are you imagining each step along the way?

_____

What criteria are you using for measuring your progress?

_____

What kind of flexibility and inner resources will you need to meet all the challenges along the way?

_____

Is your current behaviour likely to help or hinder your achievement?

Do you need to learn any new skills?

_____

Do you have a plan?

_____

How do you expect your achievement of this outcome to affect your physical environment?

_____

_____

How to get the most from this exercise

Solo. We recommend you ask an NLP practitioner to lead you through the exercise. If you do it yourself, then be absolutely honest and reflect on your past experience to answer the questions and make realistic descriptions. If you feel that there is any misalignment, then look at changing either a value or belief using the exercises in the earlier chapters.

Duo. Look and listen for any signs of incongruence. If you hear a 'yes' with the voice tone of 'I think so', then check it out with some questions. Probe any area where there is hesitation or uncertainty, but be patient also and wait for the answers. Hesitation is most likely to be noticed in the breathing and/or voice tone. When aligned, all communication will be congruent including the voice tone, breathing and body language. This is where commitment is highest and there will be an eagerness to take the first step.

CHAPTER 6

Connect and engage with rapport

Angela's story

Mike: 'I'm getting really frustrated with Angela', said Mike as he sat down for coffee with James. 'She is never there when I want her', he added.

James: 'That's odd, she always does a terrific job on my projects', replied James.

Mike: 'Are we talking about the same person?'

James: 'We only know one Angela, and she exceeds my expectations every time.'

Mike: 'Well, I've given up with her', exclaimed Mike.

Mike was Angela's line manager, but she also reported to other directors including James. Mike had similar problems with other members of his team and he would complain about their lack of attention to priorities in his area. Angela transferred to another team at the first opportunity, like others before her. Regardless of this, Mike didn't see himself as a cause of the high staff turnover in his team.

Mike took very little interest in the people in his team. He seemed to only notice when things went wrong. When things were going OK you wouldn't hear from him. In contrast, James took a sincere interest in people working on his projects. He knew he couldn't motivate people he was not line managing by rewards alone, so he built positive relationships with them. He recognised good work and made a special effort to say thank you. He offered support and had an 'open-door' policy. The result was a strong rapport between him and the people working on his projects, so that when priorities clashed, as they often did, Angela and others like her chose to work with James rather than Mike.

brilliant overview

You are about to learn:

- The purpose of rapport and how it is used
- The concept of pacing and leading
- What respect and trust have to do with rapport
- Creating rapport with yourself
- Matching and mirroring to pace and build rapport
- Pacing and leading to influence an outcome
- Creating rapport with groups
- When it might be useful to break rapport.

brilliant examples

Think of someone who you would like to get along with better – someone you want to influence or sell to, or someone whose cooperation you want to enlist. Use one of your brilliant examples from earlier chapters if appropriate, or choose someone who frustrates you, or seems to have a lack of understanding about you or your needs. In this chapter you will explore ways of interacting with this person with the aim of building a stronger relationship with them.

Write your examples here.

_____

_____

_____

_____

The purpose of rapport

Rapport is like a dance between two or more people. You can say that people have rapport with each other when they are relaxed and feeling good in the company of one other. You are at ease, and there is no sense of threat in any way, no judgement of each other, no hidden agendas, and no imposed status power. When these barriers are removed, respect and trust begin to form. What follows is a synchronisation of body language – the display of rapport.

Matching and mirroring to create rapport with others

Communication is so much more than the words. Interpretation of what a person means when they are speaking is taken from the tone of voice, facial expression, gestures and other non-verbal parts of the message. In fact, interpretation between people happens even when they are not talking. Sometimes just a look is enough. When there is strong rapport between two people, there is often a match in body position, breathing rate and muscular tension.

You can use this natural tendency of matching non-verbal communication to make communication easier and to build rapport. This will help you to 'get on the wavelength' of someone you want to influence as you will be perceived as someone who seems to be tuned in to their way of thinking.

Knowing about synchronisation of physiology you can match and mirror in order to start the rapport process. There are many ways to achieve this including:

- body posture (leaning backwards/forwards/sideways);
- head position (tilted up/down/to one side);
- legs (crossed/bent under/outstretched);
- arms (behind head/on knees/leaning/crossed);
- gestures (not at the same time, only when you are speaking);
- breathing (deep/shallow/fast/slow);
- voice (high/deep/fast/slow).

Matching is putting your body in the same position as the other person, so if they lean to the left so do you. Mirroring is doing the same with your left as they do with their right (as in a mirror image when you are facing each other). You do not need to be precise; just get close to it and be natural. You can also cross-match, so if the person you want to build rapport with is tapping with their pen, you can tap your foot to the same rhythm. Mismatching is one way to break or resist the rapport building process.

brilliant tip

For the next week watch people in public places. Notice their physiology when they are enjoying each others' company, and/or when they are in disagreement.

You may wish to build rapport with a person simply to enjoy their company, or to help the flow of communication in a work team, social group or sales process. If you want to influence anyone with whom you do not already have a good working relationship, then building rapport with them is vital. Any form of leadership or influencing requires rapport since the leader's job is to set a future direction on which others can focus their energy, and they will only do this willingly when there is rapport with the leader.

Pacing and leading

The purpose of rapport is to put yourself in a position of influence and lead with your ideas. Imagine getting 'in step' with the other person by listening and understanding them while paying attention to the way they are communicating. Hold back your agenda until you are in step, and then you can begin to lead. When you have matched for a while, you can test whether you are able to lead by changing one aspect of your body language. If the other person follows suit you are now leading the process. Pacing is about creating rapport before you begin to lead with your ideas.

 presupposition

'Resistance is a sign of a lack of rapport.'

Without rapport you are leaving your influence to chance; hoping that other people will respond positively and be persuaded by your logic. In some cases this will work for you, but only with those people with whom you already have a strong common connection. Even these people may resist your ideas and logic if you are unable to express yourself convincingly. Whenever you encounter resistance to your ideas or needs, chances are that there is a lack of rapport.

You can also pace by matching visual, auditory and kinaesthetic preferences using words and phrases such as see, imagine, view, paint me a picture, for the visual sense; feel, gripping, work it through, run it by me, warm vibes, for the kinaesthetic sense, and hear, discuss, describe, tell me the story, tune in, for the auditory sense. These words and phrases are called sensory predicates. Refer to the table (overleaf) for more sensory predicates.

Visual	Auditory	Kinaesthetic
I see what you are saying.	I hear you loud and clear.	What you're saying feels right to me.
I know it looks that way.	So I've heard.	My feelings exactly.
That's clear.	That clicks.	That fits.
That's how I see it.	That rings a bell for me.	That strikes me as correct.
That's given me a picture.	That sounds right.	I catch your drift.
It's unclear.	I can't make rhyme nor reason of it.	I'm trying to take it all in.
It's too vague.	It doesn't click.	It doesn't feel right.
I want to show you something.	I want to tell you something.	I want to put something to you.
Do you see what I mean?	Does it sound right?	Does that feel right?

exercise 6.1   Using sensory predicates

Translate the following statements into the other sensory systems as in the example given. Practice in using the various sensory systems will help you to be flexible with your communication by matching their sensory predicates.

Fill in the missing boxes in the table below.

Translate visual	Translate auditory	Translate kinaesthetic
Paint me a picture.	Describe it to me.	Run me through it.
I'm looking into it.		
	We need to stay tuned-in.	
		Grab this opportunity.
Can you see the possibilities?		
	Let me tell you how it is.	
		We need to assimilate this information.
There are too many grey areas.		
	That resonates with me.	

 **brilliant** action

Spend a day just listening to the sensory predicates people use. On the following day, focus on matching sensory predicates with the people you communicate with. Do the same for a week at a time to develop the flexibility to respond in whichever sensory predicates are being used by the people you interact with.

exercise 6.2   Rapport building

Practising rapport building is best done for real. Rapport exercises which are set up and orchestrated don't have the same impact as when you create rapport with an unsuspecting person.

1   Take a walk around a busy shopping centre and choose three shops which sell similar items. Your aim is to engage a sales assistant in each shop and practise pacing and leading.

2   When you have paced for a few minutes, switch to leading and notice if the assistant follows you. You can lead by changing your body position, for example folding your arms or leaning back slightly. If the assistant doesn't follow your lead, then do more pacing.

3   Do the same with each of the three assistants and note the differences. If you feel a little mischievous and want to buy something, see how much discount you can get simply through building rapport and then asking for a lower price.

Record your results here.

_____

_____

_____

_____

_____

_____

How to get the most out of this exercise

Solo. Watch an assistant from a distance at first, observing body language. Do they move quickly or slowly, gracefully or in quick spurts? Next move in closer and listen to the tone and speed of their voice. What aspects of the product are they emphasising the most, colour, shape, sound, features? Now ask them for some assistance. Say you are looking for a particular product and emphasise the same characteristics as you have heard them mention earlier to other customers. Add in the body language and voice tone matching and then take the lead after a few minutes.

As a variation on this exercise, make a conscious decision to build rapport with someone you know who you find awkward or puzzling in some way, maybe at work. Wait until an opportunity arises and instead of reacting the way you always have done with this person, just pace them. Notice how they react differently to you when you change your response to them.

Duo. In both these exercises you could take a friend with you to observe the interaction between the two of you. Your friend will be able to feed back the dance of rapport which takes place between you and the other person, and may notice some things you didn't pick up which you could have utilised in the matching process.

 **brilliant** tip

The next time you attend a social event, ask questions to find out as much as you can about the people you meet. Avoid talking about yourself, giving brief replies to questions which come your way. Be sincere with your curiosity, and notice how many people seem to enjoy talking about themselves, and warm to you the more you show an interest in them.

Trust

Some people are inherently trusting of others and require very little experience or evidence in order to trust. There is plenty of evidence of people being scammed and taken for a ride. People who fall for these scams give their trust rapidly, and require little evidence to do so. They usually take the position of always trusting until the other party is proven to be untrustworthy. Other people do not trust so easily, and you may need more than matching and mirroring to gain their trust and build rapport.

Leaders have learned that employees who do not trust their managers or each other are unlikely to perform well. Current research on this topic, using NLP to model trust in global virtual teams, has been conducted by John Spiers[1] of Reuters.

In any professional group there is usually a degree of trust between individuals based on a common understanding of the shared professional knowledge and principles. This is what John Spiers calls *swift trust*, in that it is given readily but can be withdrawn easily the moment one team member is let down by another. When you want to influence someone with whom you have no professional shared knowledge, such as in a sales situation, or an organisational change initiative, you need more than swift trust to strike a lasting common bond.

 **presupposition**

'Respect the other person's map of the world.'

Respect and trust are important foundations for the creation of rapport. As each and every one of us creates our own version of reality through our internal representation, we take to people who closely match our version, or who show they understand it.

---

1 'Trust in Global Virtual Teams' by John Spiers, Chapter 23 in *NLP Business Masterclass* by David Molden.

exercise 6.3   Who do you trust?

Think of someone you trust implicitly and assess the degree of rapport you have with them on a scale of 0–10, with 0 being no rapport and 10 being the highest level of rapport.

Scale of rapport =

_____

Now think of someone you don't trust and assess the degree of rapport you have with them on the same scale as above.

Scale of rapport =

_____

You will be asked to return to these scores in the next exercise.

exercise 6.4   Meta-frame

When you find yourself in a conflict with another person, and you want to regain, or create rapport, the meta-frame process will help. It utilises the alignment model (Chapter 5) and connects at the highest level of purpose. Here's an example.

> James is frustrated that his company is relocating his office which will mean extra travelling and time away from his family. The move also brings a major change to his work schedule which he disagrees with. He has been given no choice in the matter.
>
> Helen is James' line manager and empathises with him, but she has no power to influence the change. James has always been a hard worker, very conscientious, with high standards of work. Since news of the change, he has started working to a strict, contracted 9–5. Helen suspects that he is job hunting as he is sometimes hard to locate and wants James to work on a new project lasting nine months. His initial response was, 'can't you give it to someone else? I have enough to do'.

This was very uncharacteristic of James and she ended up giving the project to a less qualified person instead as she couldn't trust James while he was in his current state of mind about the company.

So what can Helen do to motivate James? There is a possibility that although James always had a good relationship with Helen he has put her in the same category as other managers he now defines as 'the company'. She needs to rebuild respect and trust with him. Referring to the logical levels model in Chapter 5, Helen can help James consider his recent behaviour at a higher level, and in this case the level of Role is probably not high enough. You can imagine a conversation regarding the nature of James' role – this is what caused his response in the first place. So we go to the level of purpose and use a meta-frame pattern such as:

James, I have noticed that since you were notified of the change, you have been acting differently towards your job. I know that you are unhappy with the circumstances imposed on you, and I empathise with you. Looking at this a different way I want you to consider one thing. You have always been totally professional and a highly valued team player, but recently I have been unable to rely on you. *James, this isn't about the company, or the change, it's about your integrity as a professional*. You know that if you don't like the new situation you have a choice, stay or leave. I really hope you will stay as you are a highly valued member of my team, but whatever you do please protect your personal integrity. You can rise above this, James; don't let a management decision affect your personal integrity.

The italicised text is the meta-frame pattern, and while Helen didn't mention his purpose, the pattern implies that while he is here his purpose for working could be to maintain his personal integrity – and not the company priorities or his rewards. Integrity rises above both these. Integrity, which was probably a value, now also becomes his purpose.

Apply this to a personal situation of your own, or use the example of the person you mistrust identified in the previous exercise. Your aim is to make a connection and begin the process of building trust.

▶

The format is very simple:

1   Describe your behaviour towards the person you mistrust:

_____

_____

_____

2   Construct a communication that implies respect and include within it a meta-frame pattern in the following structure:

This isn't about (X), it's about (Y), isn't it?

Make sure that the meta-frame (Y) is a personal value for the other person elevated to the logical level of purpose.

_____

_____

_____

_____

How to get the most out of this exercise

The aim of this exercise is to create a reframe in the way a situation is being perceived. This particular reframe takes a personal value and reframes it at the higher level of purpose, hence the name of the exercise 'meta-frame'. Whilst this technique doesn't change the situation itself, it changes the way it is being perceived and diverts the focus of attention away from the perceived negative circumstances and towards a higher purpose. In this way rapport can be regained and the trust in the relationship maintained.

Solo. This can be done on your own quite successfully. Imagine stepping up from the circumstances and feeling bigger and smarter than the people who created the situation you find yourself in. Ask yourself what's important about the work you do, and make the answer to this question your overriding purpose. Also remind yourself that you have a choice, and until you choose otherwise you are going to protect your professional integrity at all costs. This is the process of regaining rapport with yourself, and it is exactly the same process when you want to build rapport with another person.

 **brilliant** tip

Try this meta-frame, 'it's not about the circumstances, it's about me and my ability to face this situation head-on'.

Duo. When you are working with someone who has adopted a negative perspective begin by eliciting their work-related values. Ask what is important about work and turn the focus away from any values that relate to what a company 'should' do.

Creating rapport is a life skill which can be used anywhere, anytime, with anyone, and for any purpose, and the fundamental prerequisite is to respect the other person's map of the world. Having said this there is something else you need to have before you attempt any of the techniques, and that is rapport with yourself.

brilliant tip

Personal power flows to where attention goes, so while the focus is on the circumstances personal power will be low. Your aim is to refocus the attention to where there is control.

Creating rapport with yourself

Are you comfortable with who you are? Are you moderately confident in most everyday situations? Do you feel at ease being close to people and interacting with them? Can you laugh at yourself? If not, you may lack rapport with yourself. In the previous example, James began acting against his better good by compromising his professionalism, in other words, creating an internal conflict, or breaking rapport with himself.

It is not so easy to build rapport with others when you don't have rapport with yourself. The meta-frame exercise is useful if you ever experience an internal conflict.

When it might be useful to break rapport

You are probably not going to want to build rapport with everyone, and there will be many people with whom you already have a natural rapport. These techniques, matching and mirroring, pacing and leading, are for creating rapport with new people or those you have found rapport lacking for some reason. There will be times however where you may not want so much rapport.

You may have met the person who can talk for their country. They have a start button for talking, but no stop button. To avoid becoming mesmerised by their consistent chatter, you can simply interrupt them and walk away, or look at your watch and say 'I have to go; maybe later'.

Communication between people follows certain patterns. When you are creating rapport you are utilising the other person's communication process and forming a pattern which connects. When you want to disconnect, all you need do is interrupt the pattern. We can learn from children who have many ways of interrupting the communication patterns of their parents.

CHAPTER 7

The elegance of language

Paul's story

Gary: 'Paul, I'd like you to attend the conference next week – I think it will be invaluable for you.'

Paul: 'I'll do my best, Gary, but there are still a number of things I have to get done.'

Gary: 'Paul, I can't help noticing that every time there is a public event to go to you look for reasons not to go – is there something stopping you that I can help with?'

As a teenager, Paul had an accident on his motorbike which left him with a large scar down the left side of his face. After the accident, Paul returned to school where he received some playful ribbing from his mates and for a while he went along with it, enjoying the attention. Slowly, however, younger members of the school began to single him out, calling him unpleasant names.

Paul began to withdraw, spending more and more time on his own. He continued this behaviour all through university, throwing himself into his work, studying hard and leaving with a first class honours degree. Paul's reclusive behaviour began to be a problem when he landed a role in the marketing department with a large food manufacturer. He had developed a slight stutter when nervous and would avoid contact with people wherever possible, preferring to communicate by e-mail and working from home as much as he could.

Paul's behaviour was the result of an accumulated set of beliefs which were now firmly embedded in his unconscious mind. So how did this gradual 'change of personality' happen? Paul's thought process over the years went something like this:

Kids are shouting at me because of my scar.

I must be ugly.

People don't like me.

I will stay out of their way – at home or in the common room.

I will never get a girlfriend.

I won't even try.

In fact I won't even put myself in a position to get rejected.

I will distract myself with my degree.

When people speak to me, I will make sure I show my right side to them.

I am stammering – more avoidance needed – back to the books.

brilliant overview

You are about to learn:

- That language, both self-talk and conversation, is an indicator of deeper level thinking
- That the same language patterns can create stress or passion
- How to talk to yourself and others positively
- Artfully vague language techniques – the Milton model
- How to use artfully vague language to pace, lead and motivate.

Artfully vague language

Milton Erickson worked with clients similar to Paul to help them move away from their limited thinking patterns and recreate their self-esteem. He did so by pacing and leading them using what became known as 'Miltonian' or 'Artfully Vague Language'. In Chapter 4 you learnt the NLP metamodel – a questioning technique for uncovering and re-shaping language patterns that indicate limited thinking. These same language patterns can be used in a positive way to unify, encourage, motivate and engage people and to pace and lead them to a new way of thinking. For example, to pace and lead Paul you might say:

And what if there is some other way that people could be seeing you because you have a scar? Could it be that they see you as unique and interesting? Someone who is prepared to take occasional risks, and who enjoys life in the fast lane? And as you develop these ideas of uniqueness and excitement you will begin to realise that life can be very different and interesting compared with the way you have been seeing it.

This short paragraph is full of the structures you have learnt being used to pace and lead Paul from his current thinking to a new way of thinking. Notice the use of the past tense at the end, thus leaving the old way of thinking firmly in the past. The important factor here is that the recognition of Paul's current thinking builds quick rapport between Paul and his coach. If the coach had tried to suggest to Paul that his scar wasn't noticeable or that he should forget about it and get on with his life, he would have completely mismatched his view of the world and been unable to pace and lead him to a better place.

Although Miltonian Language was adopted initially in therapy, its use soon become widely appreciated in business, the sports arena and education to encourage and motivate.

▶ brilliant examples

Think of someone or a group of people you would like to bring on board with your ideas. This can be in a work context or in your home and social life. Maybe you belong to a group of volunteers outside work and are championing a cause or maybe you'd like to 'sell' an idea to your friends and family. You may want to help a friend or colleague through a difficult patch or get their buy-in to an idea. In this chapter you are going to learn how to use artfully vague language to inspire yourself and others.

Write down your real examples here.

_____

_____   ▶

_____

_____

_____

_____

_____

_____

Stress or passion?

In the story above, Paul slowly allowed the feelings that resulted from his scar to affect his thinking in a negative way until eventually reclusive behaviour took the place of his previously energetic, outgoing approach to life. Such a change can happen almost imperceptibly at first such that loved ones don't even register the change until it is firmly embedded. Using the precision language described in Chapter 3, with the support of some carefully chosen NLP techniques, could have prevented Paul from going down this slippery slope.

The same language patterns that Paul was using in a negative way to cause himself stress can be used positively to create passion and motivation. Take a look at this extract from the speech made by President Obama on the night he became the first black President of the United States of America. You may recognise some of the language patterns you learned in Chapter 4. Notice how the same patterns are being used by Obama to purposely generalise, delete and distort, resulting in an inspirational artfully vague speech.

Hello, **Chicago** [universal truth].

If there is anyone out there **who still doubts** [inclusive] that America is a place where **all things are possible** [possibility], **who still wonders** [inclusive] if **the dream** [nominalisation] of our founders is alive in our time, **who still questions** [inclusive] the power of our **democracy,** [nominalisation] **tonight is your answer** [lack of reference].

**It's the answer** [complex equivalence 1] told by **lines that stretched** [inclusive] around schools and churches in numbers this nation has **never** *[universal quantifier] seen,* **by people who waited three hours and four hours** *[complex equivalence 2],* **many for the first time in their lives** *[inclusive],* **because** *[complex equivalence]* **they** *[unspecified noun]* **believed that** *[mind-read]* **this time must be different,** *[necessity and lack of comparison] that their* **voices could be that difference** *[possibility].*

It's the answer *[lack of reference] spoken by* **young and old, rich and poor, Democrat and Republican, black, white, Hispanic, Asian, Native American, gay, straight, disabled and not disabled, Americans** *[inclusive]* **who sent** *[unspecified verb]* **a message** *[unspecified noun]* **to the world that we have never** *[universal quantifier]* **been just a collection of individuals or a collection of red states and blue states** *[inclusive].*

We are, and **always** *[universal quantifier] will* **be,** *[unspecified verb] the United States of America.*

It's the answer *[lack of reference] that* **led** *[unspecified verb]* **those who've been told** *[unspecified verb] for* **so long** *[lack of comparison] by* **so many** *[lack of comparison] to be cynical and fearful and doubtful about what* **we can achieve** *[possibility] to* **put their hands** *[unspecified noun] on the arc of history* **and bend** *[unspecified verb]* **it once more** *[presupposition] toward the hope of a* **better** *[lack of comparison] day.*

It's been **a long time** *[lack of comparison] coming, but tonight,* **because** *[cause/effect] of what* **we** *[unspecified noun]* **did** *[unspecified verb] on this date in this election at this defining moment,* **change has come to America** *[lack of reference].*

A little bit earlier this evening, I **received** *[unspecified verb] an extraordinarily gracious call from Senator McCain.*

And so the speech continues using artfully vague language to unify and excite his audience without ever touching on the policies which may cause disagreement in the crowd. President Obama knew on that night that he had to speak to the world through Chicago in a way that people would remember for a long time to come as he began the challenging role he had undertaken. To do this he made sure that not a single person could contest what he said.

Take another look at the speech – you will recognise the language patterns from Chapter 3 in brackets which relate to the highlighted sections of the text. Whatever you think of Barack Obama as a politician, he fought his way to be President of the United States using speeches designed to unite people in language that they could interpret for themselves.

exercise 7.1   **Artfully vague language practice**

Here is another extract from a very famous speech. See how many language structures you can identify and notice the similarities with the Barak Obama speech. This speech was made by Nelson Mandela at his inauguration as President of South Africa in 1994. Remember that Nelson Mandela was the first black lawyer in South Africa. He certainly knew how to be specific when cross-examining in court but he also knew, like Barak Obama, that he had to speak to the world through South Africa on that night. By using artfully vague language he was able to speak to all the factions which constituted South African society at the time without alienating any one group. Notice how he begins the speech by addressing everyone in the audience. We call this an 'all inclusive' statement – it sends the unconscious message to the audience that they are in the right place and being acknowledged for who they are. There is space at the end of each paragraph for you to write down the patterns you notice.

The speech:

Your Majesties,
Your Highnesses,
Distinguished Guests,
Comrades and Friends.

Today, all of us do, by our presence here, and by our celebrations in other parts of our country and the world, confer glory and hope to newborn liberty.

_____

_____

_____

Out of the experience of an extraordinary human disaster that lasted too long, must be born a society of which all humanity will be proud.

_____

_____

_____

Our daily deeds as ordinary South Africans must produce an actual South African reality that will reinforce humanity's belief in justice, strengthen its confidence in the nobility of the human soul and sustain all our hopes for a glorious life for all.

_____

_____

_____

All this we owe both to ourselves and to the peoples of the world who are so well represented here today.

_____

_____

_____

To my compatriots, I have no hesitation in saying that each one of us is as intimately attached to the soil of this beautiful country, as are the famous jacaranda trees of Pretoria and the mimosa trees of the bushveld.

_____

_____

_____

Artfully vague language in everyday use

Similar language is used in business today – company mission statements and values are written in this way. Politicians, board directors and public speakers who want to 'rally the troops' have learnt to speak using this type of language to motivate and inspire. Anyone with a combination of big picture and towards metaprogrammes may also be inclined to speak naturally in artfully vague language.

Here is the mission statement for Microsoft:

Our mission is to help people and businesses throughout the world realize their full potential. As the world's largest software company, Microsoft helps to create social and economic opportunities wherever we work, live, and do business.

Our technology innovations, our people, our partnerships, and our day-to-day business make a meaningful contribution to the prosperity of communities and the sustainability of the planet.

Our commitment to good corporate citizenship reflects our belief that social and economic opportunity go hand in hand. When individuals, communities, and governments thrive, so does our business. To support this cycle, we focus on the following:

- *Strengthening Economies*
- *Addressing Societal Challenges*
- *Promoting a Healthy Online Ecosystem*
- *Managing a Sustainable Business*

We are proud to partner with thousands of governments, NGOs, and companies in the more than 100 countries in which we work to help everyone achieve their full potential.

Here are the value commitments of a European haulage company, Norbert Dentressangle:

TOWARDS CLIENTS

The People in Red commit themselves to serving the performance targets of their clients. They are always ready to listen to their clients' needs and to show humility. The People in Red are accessible, reactive and innovative. They know how to adapt what they have to offer to the needs of their clients and strive daily to win their loyalty and keep their trust.

TOWARDS FELLOW EMPLOYEES

The People in Red believe in good behaviour and set high standards for themselves. They are always ready to help a colleague, share their passion for their trade and pass on their know-how. They actively seek out situations of responsibility and personal progress.

TOWARDS THE ENVIRONMENT

The People in Red are concerned by the common good. As such, they cultivate an attitude of responsibility in their profession and work to enhance the commitment to sustainable development made by the Group on a daily basis.

TOWARDS SHAREHOLDERS

The People in Red honour their commitment to their shareholders. They strive to achieve top tier economic performance in their sector and provide truthful information so that shareholders can evaluate risks accurately.

exercise 7.2   Mission statement

If you work for an organisation, make a note of its values or mission statement here and note down the language structures you recognise.

_____

_____

_____

_____

Write down exactly what this means to you in terms of the things you do at work.

_____

_____

_____

_____

_____

Now ask a colleague or colleagues to do the same below without showing them what you have written.

_____

_____

_____

_____

Do they match with your interpretation or are they different in any way?

 presupposition

'The meaning of your communication is in the response.'

If you were so inclined, you could ask a great many precision questions of the examples given above. This would give you an opportunity to compare the perceived expectations of your colleagues with the reality of the behaviours demonstrated in your organisation. In other words, is your organisation walking its talk?

Using artfully vague language in your personal life

You can use artfully vague language to pace and lead your partner, friend or family member from a place of limitation to somewhere more useful. Here is an example of pacing and leading a friend who is upset that her son constantly leaves his bedroom untidy.

Example

Cindy, it's admirable that you have such a high value around tidiness and cleanliness and I know that in later life your children will really appreciate the example you have been setting them – especially when they have children of their own. Imagine them all grown up and coming to your house with their children and their toys and games and being excited to see Grandma. What would you like your grandchildren to think of you? Is it the fun, exciting Grandma who plays creatively with them or the miserable one who keeps telling them to tidy up? How do you want your son to remember you? Do you think it might be the same? Untidiness is generally an expression of freedom – a great sign that your son is growing up and becoming independent – both traits that will serve him well in later life – isn't that great?

 tip

Use artfully vague language to **pace and lead** your friends and family towards a more **productive way of thinking**.

exercise 7.3 Influencing in action

From your brilliant examples at the beginning of this chapter, select one person from your social circle who you would like to influence in some way. Imagine that you are going to meet very soon and you have made up your mind to have a challenging conversation with them about something you may not agree on or something you would like them to do but you are not quite sure how they will react.

Using the examples given in the two speeches as a guide, write a few positive artfully vague statements to introduce and outline your case.

_____

_____

_____

_____

_____

_____

_____

How to get the best out of this exercise

Solo. Make sure you have a well formed outcome for this exercise. If necessary, refer back to Chapter 1. Arrange your sentences to pace and lead your friend or family member towards your outcome. Experiment with different alternatives and practise your results.

Duo. Use precision questioning (Chapter 4) to make sure that the explorer is clear about their outcome and all its consequences. Discuss the possibilities in relation to the language used and listen to the final version. Encourage the explorer to practise.

When you become practised at using artfully vague language, you will find yourself able to pace and lead people elegantly and effectively, avoiding showdowns and confrontation while at the same time broadening your own and other's thinking. This is the language used by coaches, sales people, politicians, marketers, advertisers, leaders, orators and just about anyone who wants to influence others in some way.

exercise 7.4 Language in everyday use

While watching television or reading magazines, begin to notice the use of this language in everyday use and write down some examples here.

_____

_____

_____

_____

_____

_____

_____

brilliant action

Why not set up a blog with some friends and invite them to continually add to your collection of examples. Ask them to notice the results of such language – does it help to change people's minds, get them to do something they previously hadn't thought of, lift their mood or take on a new perception?

Information frames

Information frames are a means of putting a metaphorical frame around a piece of information in order to keep an interaction or meeting on track and less susceptible to distraction, or lead the way for some fresh thinking. Used together with artfully vague language, they form a powerful technique for pacing and leading. Here are some examples of frames and how they can be used.

Outcome frame

This focuses on the outcome of any specific event. A common NLP answer to the question 'what should I do?' is that 'It depends on your outcome'. When we set clear outcomes for ourselves, decision-making is easier and we can behave with intention, rather than just wandering around aimlessly. The reason why so many meetings are ineffective is that people get together and start talking about things until it's time to go somewhere else. The pattern of behaviour excluded setting a clear outcome at the outset.

Relevancy frame

This helps to minimise direct digressions and distractions by challenging the input of disconnected information, e.g. 'In what way is this relevant to what we are discussing here?' or 'Can I just ask what the connection is here?'

Backtrack frame

This keeps the flow between any number of past events and the current one. Use it to pace and lead thinking and to summarise during a meeting. It establishes you as a facilitator and reminds people of past decisions.

Ecology frame

This is used to consider wider consequences of your decisions by involving all the stakeholders and pre-empting resistance to change. It also prevents unwelcome surprises, e.g. 'What are all the possible consequences of taking this action?'

Evidence frame

Use this frame to challenge generalisations and to define how you know when goals are achieved, e.g. 'What evidence supports your belief that people will readily accept this decision?' 'What evidence will measure our success in achieving this outcome?'

Contrast frame

Use to clarify the objection or difficulty in quantifiable terms by choosing a suitable scenario to use as a contrast, e.g. '£2,000 might seem like a lot of money for a life-changing personal development course, but many people spend much more than that on a holiday and any benefit disappears very quickly afterwards.'

As-if frame

Use to assess the feasibility of an idea or proposal where little evidence exists to support it. You could begin with an 'as-if' storyboard of the likely events involved with implementing an idea or proposal. Take it step by step, visualising the process and interactions between people, and identify potential problems and areas for special attention. Can be used as a technique for dissociation, e.g. 'Imagine you had already done that (task), what did you do first?'

Agreement frame

Use to set up agreed criteria for making decisions that you can refer back to if things get out of hand, e.g. 'Do you recall that we agreed up front to X?' Use also to create an agreement where a problem is perceived to be one of fundamental disagreement, e.g. 'It seems that no-one wants to agree. If that's what's preventing a decision here maybe we could reach an agreement of some kind first'.

Discovery frame

Sometimes you may want to enter into a state of curiosity and ideas creation. It is times like this that evaluation will kill the creative process, so you can avoid this by using the discovery frame, e.g. 'For the next two hours I/we are going to be totally immersed in discovery and discovery alone.' What's the most intense state of discovery you can create for you or your team?

Open frame

This removes all frames and opens up a discussion or activity to anything that anyone wants to say or do. It is very useful in training sessions and team working. Use it to deal with questions, issues, and ideas that may have been previously excluded due to contextual or time limits.

exercise 7.5   Using frames to stay on track

Next time you are at a meeting, whether a one to one with a client or colleague, or a group meeting at work, or in your private life, e.g. a charity committee meeting or a local council meeting, see how many frames you can use. It doesn't matter if you are not chairing the meeting – you can use the frames from any perspective. After the meeting write down your results here and note down the impact the frames had on the meeting,

_____

_____

_____

_____

_____

_____

Have fun using the skills in this chapter – the more you practise, the more you will find yourself in a position of influence.

CHAPTER 8

It only takes a moment

Time for Tina and John's story

Tina: 'Are you coming, John? It's 5.30!'

John: 'I'll be there in a sec, I just want to make one last call – I'll catch you up.'

Tina: 'John, you are always the last to finish!'

Tina and John work in the same call centre performing similar roles. They are part of a customer service team for a national retail chain. Their work is rewarded by bonuses paid on targets related to the number of calls they deal with each day. They both receive similar bonuses at the end of each quarter although their approach to their work appears to be very different. To watch John work, you would think he had all the time in the world – arriving at work in the nick of time, settling himself down having grabbed a cup of coffee and chatted to a couple of colleagues on the way. He didn't seem to mind how long he chatted to each customer; they received his full attention and invariably his calls ended in an amicable solution. Some calls took just a few minutes, others seemed to ramble on at length but John remained unperturbed. He rarely looked at his watch during the day and took his lunch break regardless of how many calls he had handled. At approximately 5.30, he rounded off his last call and left the building.

Tina approached her work in a more methodical way. She arrived at work early enough to ensure that she had time to visit the cloakroom, make a coffee, make a plan for the day and prepare herself mentally before answering the telephone. Tina knew exactly how long she could spend on each call and would make sure that her calls did not exceed this allotted time. If she thought a call was going to go over time she would find some way of winding up the conversation quickly so that she could move on to her next call. When 5.30 arrived, she would remove her headphones and leave them ready for the next day.

 overview

You are about to learn:

● How different people code time

● What impact such coding has on our lives

● The sequential nature of time and of time lines

● How we perceive people with different time lines from our own

● How to elicit your own time line

● How to change your time line to increase flexibility

● How to save time by changing the way you feel about what you do.

We all perceive time differently

In the scenario of Tina and John, above, watching these two people at work, you would notice the differences in their approach and may even make a judgement as to their professionalism depending on your own perception – but both are achieving positive results. The way each person perceives time has an impact on the way they go about their work, and their life.

brilliant examples

Write a list of things you do over a set period of time. This can be a day, week, fortnight or a month. Include all the different tasks that you carry out between waking up and bedtime. Give each item a value according to how much you enjoy completing this activity. On a scale of 1–10, with 10 being the most enjoyable, place your score against each item as follows:

- 9–10   Thoroughly enjoyable
- 7–8   Reasonably enjoyable
- 5–6   Indifferent
- 3–4   Dislike doing
- 1–2   Avoid if I can

Activity   Enjoyment score

_____

_____

_____

_____

_____

_____

_____

_____

_____

Why do some people appear to 'manage time well' while others appear to 'have no concept of time'?

If you look at the heading of this section, it is, of course, ridiculous. No one can 'manage time' and to 'have no concept of time' means you could never get anywhere ever on time unless you happen to be lucky. Both phrases are metaphors for how we perceive time. There are 24 hours in every day and there is nothing we can do to stop the passing of time, and we haven't yet found a way of creating more. So why have so many timely expressions found their way into language? Time flies, that's a waste of time, I don't have the time, time stops for no-one, time honoured way, are all expressions which actually have a much deeper meaning that indicates something more than the passing of time:

Time flies – *I didn't make this particular thing a priority.*
That's a waste of time – *I don't value what you are suggesting.*
I don't have the time – *I don't want to.*
Time stops for no-one – *You had better hurry up and get on with it.*
Time honoured way – *We have always done it like this.*
I'm rushing to meet this deadline – *I'm out of control.*

In Chapter 2 you were introduced to the In-time/Through-time meta-programme and you probably recognised John in our story above as having an in-time pattern and Tina as having a through-time pattern. Both have managed to make their concept of time work well for them in their working environment and as long as they respect each other's way of working there should be no problems. Issues can arise when people begin to make judgements and put meanings on what appears to them to be peculiar or unnatural behaviour.

To understand your perception of time let's take a moment to explore your own personal time line.

exercise 8.1   Eliciting a time line

This exercise, and the concept of 'time line' can be compared with Albert Einstein's concept of space-time, i.e. you can only really know time by its relationship to space. So the future is ahead in space, and the past is behind. This concept helps us to be more aware of how we relate to the passing of time, and the sequence of events in space-time, or a time line. Read the exercise through first so you can commit it to memory, then sit quietly with your eyes closed and follow the directions below.

You are going to access some memories from different stages of your life as follows:

Something that happened –

● when you were five or six years old;

- 10 years ago;
- five years ago;
- last week.

Something you are intending to do –

- next week;
- next month;
- in six months' time;
- next year.

As you access these memories, notice from which direction they appear in your mind. Are they coming in from behind, from one side or from the front somewhere? If you were to plot them on a piece of paper and join up the dots, what would they look like?

Solo. It is possible to do this alone although much easier with a facilitator. Sit quietly and relax with your eyes closed. As you allow the memories to arrive, notice the direction, height and distance from which they appear. When you have a sequence of past and future memories, mentally join them together in a line to establish your time line.

Duo. Facilitate this exercise by asking the explorer to recall past and future memories and to point to the direction in which they appear. Draw a circle on a piece of paper to represent the explorer's head looking down from the top and plot each memory in relation to the head as it appears. When finished, join the dots to create a time line representation.

Time lines can take many shapes and forms. Overleaf are two common time lines.

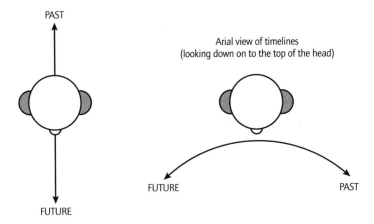

PAST

FUTURE

Arial view of timelines
(looking down on to the top of the head)

FUTURE   PAST

There is no right or wrong way to perceive time and sometimes your time line will work well for you and sometimes it won't. Generating flexibility around your perception of time will enable you to make the most of both ends of the continuum, i.e. to be in-time when the situation demands and through-time when planning and organisation are required. How would it be if you could be in-time while coaching a colleague, helping a friend through a traumatic experience, relaxing on holiday or solving a business or personal problem and then revert to through-time when planning your day, week, month, children's parties, business strategy or holiday calendar?

exercise 8.2   Becoming more through-time

If you have something resembling the classic in-time line illustrated above, you may find that one or more of the following apply:

- You find difficulty estimating the amount of time needed for tasks and journeys.

- Others are frustrated by your apparent lack of reverence to your lateness.

- You find it difficult to remember events beyond a day or two past.

- You cannot see too far into the future.

- You agree to do too much because you find difficulty assessing how much time things take – you try to squeeze everything into 'now'.

● Your friends sometimes feel undervalued by you because you arrive late for engagements.

In order to benefit from this exercise, you need to have a good reason for doing it. Explore your values around this change – what is it that is so important to you that you won't achieve if you don't develop an alternative time line? Is it connected to a relationship, a career change, a promotion, a work related strategy or a decision you have been procrastinating over? Whatever it is, be clear about your intention so that your will to change is strengthened by the ultimate outcome.

Write down your purpose for this change.

_____

_____

_____

_____

_____

1   Sit quietly where you won't be disturbed and close your eyes.

2   Imagine a line stretching from left to right in front of you. Try different distances to see which works best for you; start with a few inches, then a foot, maybe a few meters out. You can give the line some form if you wish – colour, texture, width.

3   Relax and bring to mind a pleasant memory of something which happened when you were a youngster. Recall the image in full detail, make it bright, put a frame around it and place it a short way in from the beginning of your imaginary time line.

4   Repeat step 3 for another four or five images at various stages of your life until you arrive at the present day, the point on the line which is right in front of you.

5   Now do the same for the future. Create an image for something significant you are going to do tomorrow and place it just a little further up the line towards the future.

6   Repeat this exercise creating as many new pictures for significant things that are coming up in the future as you can.

▶

7 Go back over your line and get a sense of the distance between the images.

8 Now create vivid images for each day next week. When you want to know what you are doing next Thursday, pull up your visual time line and focus on your image for Thursday.

Changing your time line in this way will add to your flexibility – you will still be able to revert to your in-time line when you feel it is appropriate.

Solo. Make sure you find a quiet space where you can do this exercise uninterrupted. Be meticulous in your creation of each image. Give your time line a structure – width, texture, colour and anything else that appeals to you.

Duo. Help the explorer to create the images by using artfully vague language to create and place each image on a time line pre-created by the explorer. Resist the temptation to suggest content – stick to the process and use your sensory acuity to know when to move on to the next stage.

 exercise 8.3   Becoming more in-time

If you have what resembles a classic through-time line then you may find one or more of the following apply:

- You become frustrated if you are late for engagements and may even feel uncomfortable for the rest of the day.

- You find in-time people frustrating especially if your timescales depend on them in some way.

- You may even refer to in-timers as disrespectful.

- Your need for a timescale is sometimes more important than the events arranged within it.

- You sometimes find it difficult to relax because you are concerned with what you are going to do next or maybe even reviewing what you did yesterday.

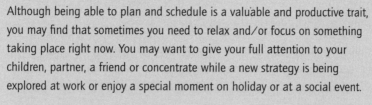

Although being able to plan and schedule is a valuable and productive trait, you may find that sometimes you need to relax and/or focus on something taking place right now. You may want to give your full attention to your children, partner, a friend or concentrate while a new strategy is being explored at work or enjoy a special moment on holiday or at a social event.

Make sure that you have a reason for doing this exercise – write down your reasons and the benefits you expect from developing this time line.

_____

_____

_____

_____

1   Get into the habit of writing the things you have to remember on an imaginary post-it note and pinning them on an imaginary board which you can access any time you wish. This is a great NLP memory jogger technique.

2   When you feel the need to be in-time, take a deep breath and push the imaginary notice board to the boundaries of your peripheral vision where you can just about see it.

3   Focus your attention outwards instead of inside your head, relax and pay attention to what is going on now, feeling confident that you can re-access your notice board any time you choose to.

4   You can also use your watch as a reminder – take it off when you want to be in-time.

Time is an emotional issue

Most time management programmes focus on arranging activities using a coding system – these can be based on colours, importance and relevance or an alphabetical system to denote the order in which things should be done. Such programmes suit through-timers admirably because time is important and deserves focus – but, of course, they don't really need the programme because they have an in-built ability to organise and plan. In-time people often attend with all good intention and start off well, planning their time effectively. However, it doesn't normally take much to throw them off course, abandon their planning and attend the programme again when next the opportunity arises.

This next section explores the connection between time and emotion. In the learning example at the beginning of this chapter you were asked to score the things you do in relation to the level of enjoyment you experience.

The FD's story

Catherine was the finance director of an international company. In a workshop we asked her to list the activities she gets involved in and to rate them in the way shown at the beginning of this chapter. We asked her about an activity which she had scored very low. She shrugged her shoulders and said 'it's not important, it's just a niggle'. Probing further we discovered that this activity required her to access some statistics from one particular department with which she had developed a strained relationship. The process would go something like this:

1 Call the department for figures.

2 Figures not ready.

3 Frustration.

4 Bang down the telephone.

5 Put task to one side.

6 Next day call department again – figures still not ready.

7 Bang down the telephone.

8 Put task to one side.

9 Next day (deadline arrived) call department – figures still not ready.

10 Get cross, throw weight around.

Catherine estimated that this whole process would take about one and a half hours in total and, as she had to do this three times a month, a task that should take a few minutes was actually taking four and a half hours. When asked how she felt about the department who were required to produce the figures she used words such as incompetent, useless, unfocused and uncaring. When asked when she last visited this department, she said: 'Two years ago!'

Remember this was just one niggle in the course of a month – imagine if Catherine had three niggles. Do the sums and you begin to realise that Catherine could be losing a day and a half a month on things that could be easily resolved. She resolved the situation simply by paying a visit to the department and re-building her relationships with the people involved. Her negative emotions which built up over time had kept her stuck in her views and unable to achieve the results she desired until she made a determined effort to break the pattern.

 **action**

Time is an **emotional issue** – what we do with it depends on a combination of factors including **personal values and your metaprogramme profile, your experience and your perceptions**. Use your **metaprogramme profile** to gain some insight into what you do with your time.

The connection between metaprogrammes and time

What do you spend your time doing? Metaprogrammes can have a significant impact on the way you organise your time. The following are some examples.

Metaprogramme combinations	Ways in which you could be using your time unproductively
External reference + Away from	Seeking feedback, focusing on the negative and mentally putting self down
Options + Considering	Reviewing all the options and then considering the implications of each one – extreme procrastination
Detail + Considering	Considering the detailed implications of taking action before getting started
External reference + Others	Looking after other people's interests – often unnecessarily
Big picture + Options	Having grand ideas but not necessarily carrying them through
Procedures + Doing	Doing repetitive things – sometimes without checking their current validity
Options + Difference	Exploring numerous new ways of doing things just because you can
Procedures + Detail	Being pedantic about things which in the bigger scheme of things have little importance
Independent + Self	Working alone and possibly missing key factors which may save you time
Internal reference + Independent	Ignoring feedback and working on obsolete data
Sameness + Procedure	Being unwilling to take on new time-saving approaches to things
Internal reference + Detail	Micromanaging

exercise 8.4   Exploring time barriers

1 Take something you rated as 1–2 on your list.

2 Explore whether your metaprogramme profile may be having an impact on your reluctance to get this done.

3 Ask yourself what it is that stops you from enjoying this activity. Here are some suggestions:

   ● It makes you feel bad because …

   ● You don't believe you have the skill set.

   ● The activity conflicts with your personal values.

   ● The activity conflicts with a metaprogramme, e.g. too much detail.

   ● You don't see a positive purpose in the activity.

   ● You have a poor relationship with other stake holders.

Write down your findings here.

_____

_____

_____

_____

_____

4 Make a plan to either:

   ● stop doing it particularly if it has no value;

   ● find a value or a purpose in it;

   ● delegate it to someone else;

   ● improve your relationships;

   ● learn the necessary skills.

Write your plan here.

_____

_____

_____

_____

▶

Solo. This exercise is best carried out over a period of time as you become more aware of the things you do in the course of your daily life and explore your reasons for the changes you would like to make. Use techniques such as the New Behaviour Generator, Values Elicitation, Belief Change and Anchoring to help you make quick effective changes.

Duo. Use meta model precision questioning to help the explorer discover the emotions held around time management. Use the techniques mentioned above to help the explorer make the required changes.

CHAPTER 9

Personal strategies for success

Nadine's story

Helen: 'How's the social entrepreneurship coming along?'

Nadine: 'Ah, I still have some things to complete before I can start.'

Helen: 'So do you have a plan?'

Nadine: 'Not completely, it's still taking shape. I have more to do first.'

Helen: 'Well, you have been talking about this for years now. Surely you are going to make a start soon?'

Nadine: 'I really want to; it's just that things keep cropping up.'

Nadine was feeling unfulfilled in her job but she had been inspired by women entrepreneurs and wanted to be like them. She wanted to build something that would have a positive effect for underprivileged children in poor areas of the country. Whilst Nadine was energised at the thought of doing something for others, she procrastinated over taking the first step. She had no worries about security, and certainly no lack of ideas, energy or compassion. She just seemed to lack the drive to make it happen.

Many people have great ideas but get stuck somewhere between the idea and action. To discover the cause of Nadine's lack of action, or any idea which isn't progressing to your desired outcome, we can break down the thought process to identify exactly what needs to change.

 **brilliant** overview

You are about to learn:

- How to change and design personal strategies
- Understanding distractions and loops
- Exercises to change a strategy that isn't working in your best interest.

How, not why

Everything you do begins with a single thought which leads to others and eventually some action may be taken. When this works all is fine, but when you are unhappy with the results you may feel angry, incompetent, inadequate or simply frustrated. Think of your thought process as a strategy – it's the way you approach a certain endeavour. It's the 'how' of getting something done. Individuals have unique strategies for a diverse range of behaviour such as procrastinating, feeling bad, over-eating, laziness, damaging a relationship with a parent, partner or one of your children, or creating anxiety, stress or lethargy. You can fix these problems when you focus on the strategy – **how** you are generating the behaviour. People often get stuck because they are asking **why**, and this tends to make things worse. Asking **why** usually results in reasons and excuses, and at the worst blaming someone or something, quite possibly yourself. When you can put your finger on exactly **how** you are causing the unwanted results then you can build more choices to help you succeed.

brilliant examples

Think of something which you have told yourself you are going to achieve, but repeated attempts have left you frustrated. Or choose something you really want to do or stop doing but the thought or idea never makes it to action. Here is a list of the kind of things you might like to change:

Learning the specific process you use to:

- feel bad, anxious, sad, depressed, stressed, guilty, regretful or lethargic;

- procrastinate;
- confuse yourself;
- limit your ability to learn;
- get angry;
- become distracted;
- smoke tobacco;
- drink too much alcohol;
- damage a relationship;
- miss deadlines;
- make poor decisions;
- feel embarrassed or intimidated;
- lack confidence;
- lose focus;
- be shy;
- be too serious, lacking fun and lightness;
- limit your results in any (specific) area of your work.

Follow the directions here, bearing in mind that the examples provided are unlikely to fit your experience exactly. Because every person has a unique personal map, the results will also be unique. Keep your specific example in mind as you read through the chapter and take your time to unpick each element of your strategy.

What is a strategy?

A strategy is the sequence of steps in a person's thoughts and feelings which result in a specific behaviour or mental ability. The strategy will be driven by a personal value and associated beliefs. You can discover any strategy by questioning a person (or yourself) to ascertain the sequence of steps used to demonstrate a cognitive ability or behaviour. Cognitive ability could be a creative thinking process or the ability to be confused. The word ability in this context does not imply a positive effect. A person can make himself ill, stressed or confused, i.e. he is able to do it using a specific strategy he may or may not be aware of.

 **tip**

The next time you catch yourself being dissatisfied with a result, rather than feeling bad and asking why, be curious to know the specific steps you went through to become dissatisfied. Where did your dissatisfaction begin? Seek to learn and identify your strategy.

What does a strategy include?

All strategies will have a unique mix of the following:

● personal values;

● metaprogrammes;

● beliefs;

● physiology;

● internal representations (visual/auditory/kinaesthetic/internal dialogue/olfactory/gustatory);

● voice characteristics.

There will also be a sequence of individual steps to mental activity and behaviour which can include one or many operations as described below using something called the TOTE model.

The TOTE model

The TOTE model simply describes the minimum number of steps in a strategy required to achieve a mental state or behaviour. It stands for:

Test – **O**perate – **T**est – **E**xit

There is always a trigger which initiates the strategy, and then a sequence of tests and operations until the strategy is complete (at the exit point).

Consider the strategy you might use for buying a new pair of shoes. The trigger could be:

● You discover a hole in your shoe.

● Your shoes begin to look shabby.

- You buy a new suit and decide you need some new shoes to go with it.

- You are in the high street and see a pair of shoes in a shop window.

- Someone tells you that you could do with a new pair of shoes.

Your personal strategy for buying shoes may last five minutes or it could last for weeks. The length of the strategy will depend upon the number of steps. Imagine someone who really needs a pair of shoes, prefers a classic design and has a high value on getting a bargain. This person might need to see and try on many pairs of shoes before all the decision criteria are met. Another person simply chooses a pair of shoes from a website in 10 minutes. Hence two people with the same objective can go about achieving it in very different ways, with very different efficiencies and results. The same happens with more important decisions including finding a career, a partner, or a new business opportunity.

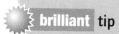 **brilliant** tip

Whatever you want to change about yourself, begin by asking 'how do I know when to do this?' Find the trigger and you are half-way to making a change.

Here's a diagram showing the various steps in the TOTE model.

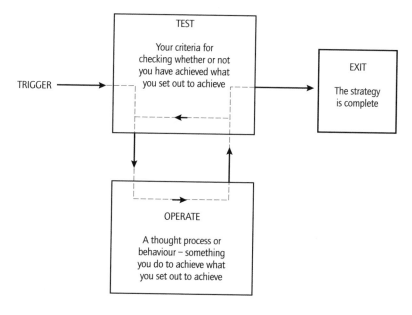

Trigger

This is the stimulus that starts the strategy which you may or may not be aware of at the time. It's usually an automatic response to something, for example you see a pair of shoes in a shop window and you just have to have them. Deciding to go for a run because you are feeling heavy is a conscious trigger, i.e. you are aware of having made a choice, whereas responding angrily to someone is more automatic.

exercise 9.1   Locating the trigger to a strategy

Take your personal example (which we shall refer to as X) and ask yourself the following questions:

How do you know when to start doing X?

_____

_____

What's the very first thing that you do when you start doing X?

_____

_____

When have you done X?

_____

_____

Is there a particular context where X happens?

_____

_____

Are there contexts where X has never happened?

_____

_____

If you want to make a change to your strategy, the best place to do this is at the trigger point. Some strategies have multiple trigger points. Take smoking as an example and ask 'how do you know when to smoke?' – after a meal; after coffee; when stressed; before bedtime; when driving; etc.

In our story at the start of this chapter, Nadine is asked, 'how do you know when to procrastinate?'

Answer: 'When I think of all the things I want to do and start to feel overwhelmed, then I don't know where to start' – this is Nadine's trigger.

Now we need to break this down into smaller chunks by asking 'how do you think about all those things you want to do?'

As Nadine answers this question, we observe her physiology, especially her eyes. We may notice that she accesses images of all the things she wants to do, or she may describe them to herself using internal dialogue. Perhaps she just feels there is much to do but she hasn't been specific about exactly what those things are.

We can also ask if there are any contexts where she thinks about her desire and doesn't end up feeling overwhelmed. If the answer is yes, this might provide information we can use later when modifying the strategy.

Test

The test is how you know when you have achieved your objective. Sometimes a strategy is ineffective because the success criterion, or test, is not well formed. In Chapter 1 you learned how to create a well-formed outcome with sensory evidence of success. Some people set themselves goals without forming a clear image of success and end up making poor distinctions and decisions. This can result in cycling through the Test-Operate loop many times as it seems no matter what you do your test is not working very well. A classic example of this is when a person decides they have had enough of their current job, perhaps due to a difficult manager, and goes for a job with a new company. They know what job they don't want, but are driven by avoidance rather than a specific future job role, so the test is very vague – just another job. As a result, they get another job, but the loop continues because from day one in the new job they are questioning whether they made the right choice. There is no exit to the strategy, just a confused and unmotivated employee.

Your test needs to be clear. How will you know when you have achieved your outcome? What will you see, hear, read and feel?

Operate

An operation can be a thought process or behaviour. In our story Nadine performed many operations in her attempt to become a social entrepreneur. She directed her efforts to under-privileged children in her country, and has a mental image of this. She attended seminars and joined a support network.

One problem some people have is that they keep performing the same OPERATION and expecting different results.

 **brilliant** presupposition

'If you always do what you have always done, you will always get what you have always had.'

---

exercise 9.2   **Discovering a TOTE loop**

What have you done so far to achieve your outcome in relation to X?

_____

_____

What's the first thought you had following the trigger?

_____

_____

What followed this thought? Was it another thought or an action?

_____

_____

How did these specific thoughts appear to you, with images and sounds?

_____

_____

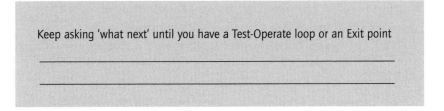

Keep asking 'what next' until you have a Test-Operate loop or an Exit point

Exit

The exit is the end of the strategy. No more operations are required and the outcome is achieved. The strategy may run again the next time there is a trigger, and some strategies, such as knowing when to smoke a cigarette, run very frequently.

Distractions and loops

There are many distractions in life which can cause you to get stuck in a loop. It's a wonder sometimes how anything is achieved. Consistent achievers have strategies that work efficiently with few distractions, and they rarely get stuck in loops.

In our story, Nadine's loop had been going on for years with no sign of an exit in sight. One distraction was her OPTIONS and IN-TIME meta-programme combination, causing her to think up lots of ways she could help under-privileged children, and then becoming confused as to where to begin. She would think of all these options at the same time, causing her to feel overwhelmed.

The following are all causes of distraction and serve to keep people cycling around loops with no EXIT:

- An overly strong metaprogramme. *Any strong metaprogramme, or combination of two or more – refer to Chapter 2. A typical combination of DETAIL and PROCEDURE results in a drive for perfection. Perfectionists are rarely satisfied and so rarely EXIT their TOTES.*

- A value conflict. *Value conflicts lead to indecision and restricted effort. A person who works for a debt collection company with a value for compassion and fairness may find it difficult to do certain tasks. This will create loops with no EXIT.*

● Lack of skill or know-how. *No matter how well you have defined your aim, or TEST, without the necessary skills you can loop around TEST-OPERATE forever. You may complete a task but feel that it was a fluke, or you didn't do it properly. Just because a task is completed it doesn't mean the loop has stopped cycling. Whenever you find yourself saying 'I should have …' instead of 'I could have …', your loop is still open. The words 'should have' imply regret, so you keep reminding yourself of what you should have done. When you use the words 'could have' it is more oriented to the next time you have to do the task.*

● Poorly defined outcome. *If you are unable to tell when you have achieved your aim, then loops keep looping. A typical example is a sales executive who finds it difficult to achieve sales. A sales executive with 12 prospects may have 12 loops running because he hasn't learned to define outcomes for his interactions with them. He is hoping that with enough information and rapport his prospects will eventually buy something from him. Effective sales executives have well-defined outcomes for every phone call, email and visit with a client.*

● Habitual (reactive) thinking and behaviour. *We are all creatures of habit, but some habits are useful whilst others are not. Habits can extend loops which you may not be aware of, and the way to get out of one of these loops is to be more aware of what you are doing – to recognise the habit and then change it.*

Running loops with no EXIT can seriously drain your energy. The more loops you are running, the more energy you are using, and the more distracted you become. Many loops are outside conscious awareness, but the mind is dwelling on them nevertheless. The more efficient your loops, the less energy you use and the more productive you are. This is the real key to productivity and effectiveness – identifying and dealing with distractions so that you can achieve results with the minimum number of OPERATIONS.

exercise 9.3   Finding the cause of a loop

Refer to your learning example X and identify the cause of any loops which run and don't EXIT. Pay attention specifically to:

Strong metaprogrammes

_____

Personal values and value conflicts related to X

_____

Your beliefs about X

_____

The submodalities of your internal representations relating to X

_____

Changes in your physiology relating to X

_____

Lack of skill or know-how relating to X

_____

Poorly defined outcome relating to X

_____

Any habitual thinking or behaviour relating to X

_____

Different ways of using strategies

So far you have been learning to use strategies to be more aware of when things are not going the way you want them to go. The purpose has been to identify the steps in a strategy so that you can change it using an NLP technique.

Changing a strategy

Once you know your strategy, the next step is to make a change so that the strategy either works better for you or has a different desired result. You might want to change your initial response to the trigger, make the trigger powerless, redefine your outcome and test, or change one or more operations. From this point on, what you do is entirely down to your creativity, deciding which technique/s to use at which stage of the TOTE.

In our story, Nadine's test is unclear, which is making her hesitate. Defining a **Well-formed Outcome** would be a good place for Nadine to start. From here she will need to outline the first stages of her plan, and a **New Behaviour Generator** technique will help her to assimilate the first steps. Her need for choices can be built into her plan once she has taken the initial steps. Then she can **build a strong positive feeling** in connection with the first outcome in her plan.

 **brilliant** tip

When you meet someone with a skill or ability you admire, ask 'how do you do that'? Then be patient as you listen and observe the entire neurophysiology reveal the strategy to you. Stay curious.

Designing a strategy

This is one of the really fun applications of NLP – designing your own strategy to achieve something, from having a better memory to being a smarter business person. Now you know how you create your unique map of the world you can configure it any way you like.

exercise 9.4   Design a strategy

First of all, decide on a strategy you would like to have. Examples might include:

- having a terrific memory
- making smart decisions
- being patient
- having enough persistence to make an idea work
- improving your sports performance
- being a great mum/dad/brother/sister/partner/friend
- being able to relax
- motivating yourself
- getting physically fit
- eating healthily
- becoming a non-smoker (having healthy lungs)
- getting things done
- achieving a happy work/life balance (or weave)
- effective studying
- learning a new language.

At the end of this exercise you should feel very confident about your strategy working for you over the long term. Once you have decided on a strategy you would like, work through each of the following steps. We will refer to your strategy as X.

1 Create a well-formed outcome for your strategy (refer to Chapter 1).

2 Create strong values for doing X (refer to Chapter 5).

3 Take on positive beliefs about X that support the values you created in step 2 (Chapter 4).

4 Imagine doing X. Make your image big, bright and colourful. Tell yourself why doing X is important to you (in a tone of voice congruent with X). Notice your feelings and make them stronger. Run through this VAK strategy a number of times and focus on it frequently throughout the day (new behaviour generator).

▶

5   Add the physiology of doing X – postures, gestures, muscle tension.

6   How do you feel now as a person who does X? Connect with this feeling and become familiar with it. It is shaping your identity as a person who does X.

7   Design a 'bring it on' state and anchor it so you can access it whenever you want to do X (Chapter 3).

How to get the most out of this exercise

When you get down to the design process you may find you have values or beliefs which are not aligned with your outcome, and will therefore limit your success. You may have current strategies that are strong enough to prevent the new one from taking hold. This is all part of the learning process you go through when acquiring a new skill and in this book you have more than enough techniques to deal with self-imposed limitations like these.

Solo. You need a good degree of self-discipline and NLP skill to design your own strategies. If you have not done this before, see if you can find a practitioner to guide you through the steps.

Duo. Look for signs of congruence at each step in the process. Ensure that beliefs are positively oriented, i.e. what I believe *will* happen, not *won't* happen.

brilliant presupposition

'If it's possible for one person, it's possible for me
(as long as I am prepared to live with the consequences).'

CHAPTER 10

Modelling excellence

The top performing store manager

Derek: 'Chris, what is it that makes this store so successful? This is one of the most deprived areas in the country and yet the sales figures consistently outshine even the most affluent areas.'

Chris: 'The secret, Derek, is in the level of enjoyment – keep staff and customers happy and engaged and not only will they work hard, they stay with you longer and absenteeism is kept to a minimum – come and spend a day with me and I will show you what I mean.'

 **overview**

You are about to learn:

- How to model excellence
- That excellence can be found in those close to you – you don't have to look to superstars and public figures for excellence.

n the *McKinsey Quarterly* an article recently appeared under the heading: 'How we do it: three executives reflect on strategic decision making'. Here is what it said about Sir Martin Sorrell:

[He] experiments, is open to intuition, and listens to flashes of inspiration. Also that he is rigorous, runs the analyses, sucks up all the data, and includes some formal processes as well.

Study the heading closely and you will see that this is not 'how' they do what they do, but simply 'what' they do.

Modelling with NLP gives you the ability to study a person's mental strategies and actual behaviour. For example, how does Sir Martin Sorrell construct his imagery? What does he say to himself, and in what tone of voice? What values and beliefs are driving this sequence? What metaprogrammes are behind his strategy? How does his physiology support this process? How does he know when enough analysis is enough? How much data is sucked up, and how does he suck it up? What formal processes are required and how does he evaluate their relevance? What metaphors is he working from?

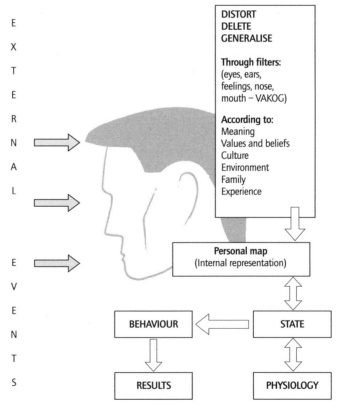

EXTERNAL EVENTS

DISTORT
DELETE
GENERALISE

Through filters:
(eyes, ears,
feelings, nose,
mouth – VAKOG)

According to:
Meaning
Values and beliefs
Culture
Environment
Family
Experience

Personal map
(Internal representation)

BEHAVIOUR

STATE

RESULTS

PHYSIOLOGY

**HOW WE FILTER INFORMATION AND PRODUCE OUR
OWN UNIQUE MAP OF THE WORLD**

In Chapter 9 you learnt how to discover strategies with the objective of either changing negative ones or copying productive ones. Modelling is the process of eliciting a series of strategies which contribute to excellent performance and observing the person doing what it is they are excellent at. People are unique and in NLP we describe this as having a 'unique map of the world' from which we communicate with others. The diagram on page 190 shows how this map is made up and includes all the aspects we have been discussing in this book. It is this unique map that determines what we think, what we do, what states we manage to achieve and ultimately our results. It makes sense therefore to 'copy' or model the thinking and behaviour patterns of people who are successful in an arena where we would like to achieve success ourselves.

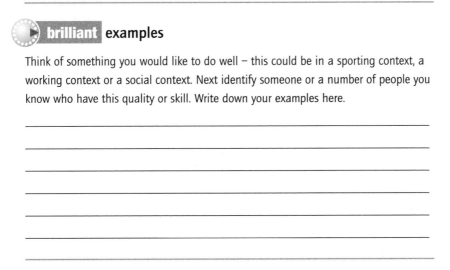

brilliant examples

Think of something you would like to do well – this could be in a sporting context, a working context or a social context. Next identify someone or a number of people you know who have this quality or skill. Write down your examples here.

_____

_____

_____

_____

_____

_____

When Derek modelled Chris

When Derek modelled Chris he discovered a consistent thinking pattern about people that went like this:

People –

- like to be valued;
- like to be trusted;
- will perform well if taught effectively;

- will rise to a challenge if encouraged;
- like to have fun;
- like to work hard;
- like to see you get your hands dirty;
- will follow whatever example you set;
- once competent like to be left to get on with the job.

These beliefs led Chris to behave in a certain way in his store. Here are some examples:

- He designed competitions for the staff to take part in and made sure that he was on the losing team so that they could nominate a forfeit for him. One such forfeit included doing the ironing for the staff. Chris took the opportunity to invite the local press to watch as he conducted his ironing activities in front of the shop. Needless to say sales soared that day.

- He trusted the staff to do their jobs. Derek noticed that he paid no attention to a known shop lifter Chris identified in the store, saying that the staff would deal with it and they did.

- He spent a good proportion of his time on the shop floor engaging the staff in conversation about their week-ends, their families and their hobbies, making them feel valued members of the team.

- When necessary he would lend a hand in the unloading bays or on the shop floor replenishing shelves although most of the time this was well covered as staff absenteeism was very low.

- He identified the strengths in his staff members and ensured that they were given roles that enabled them to excel.

Derek noticed Chris's ability to scan the shop floor, taking account of the overall layout and appearance while also talking to individual members of staff about their particular areas of responsibility. He gave just the right feedback to those who needed it and refrained from doing so for those who didn't. In fact, he noticed Chris's flexibility across a range of metaprogrammes. He also noticed his ability to quickly build rapport with both his staff and customers and to make people feel special. Chris's absenteeism rates and staff turnover rates were low, a factor which contributed significantly to the profitability of the store.

Derek was able to model Chris while he accompanied him around the store, observing from a short distance. Being able to observe a person in action will give you better quality information for your model. However, this is not always possible and you may have to rely totally on your ability to ask questions and on your sensory acuity.

Compare Chris's model with that of a low-performing store manager – Nigel

Nigel had a different view of his role. He operated a regime of tight control and management. His beliefs included:

- The staff need managing.
- If I don't watch them I will not spot their mistakes.
- I need to look at all the sales and performance figures on a daily basis and make sure that people are aware of their targets.
- Work is serious.
- I have no control over the performance of the store in this economic climate.

Nigel's thinking resulted in the following behaviours:

- Carrying around reams of printed reports which he referred to occasionally.
- Getting other people to do things for him even though prevailing circumstances suggested he was best positioned for the job.
- Acting as the store security officer.
- Limiting 'fun' type activities which did not fit his perception of serious work.

In contrast to Chris's store, the atmosphere in Nigel's was austere and customers appeared to enter the store, buy what they needed and retreat at the earliest opportunity. Nigel's absenteeism and staff turnover rates were also very high, causing frequent costly recruitment, temporary staff cover and staff training, all of which affected his profitability.

What to model

Modelling is used in business to create models of excellence in areas such as customer service, sales, leadership, management, negotiating and recruitment. Models are generated from best performers and taught to colleagues to raise performance throughout whole teams. Modelling is also used in teaching and sports. If you want the perfect golf swing, backhand in tennis, drop kick in rugby then find someone who performs consistently well and model their thinking and behaviour around these skills.

exercise 10.1   Modelling an exemplar

Write down the skill you would like to have and the names of one or more people who have it. These people will be your exemplars.

_____

_____

_____

_____

_____

Arrange to meet these people, one at a time, and ask them if they would be prepared to answer some questions about their skill and have you shadow them while they are doing it.

Modelling your exemplar

Here are the questions to ask.

Belief questions

- What do you believe about success?
- What do you believe about your own ability to succeed?
- What do you believe about your outcomes?
- What thoughts go through your head when things don't go to plan?

Values questions

- What is important to you about your success?
- What else is important to you?

- What else?
- What else?

You may even carry out a values elicitation here as described in Chapter 5 to find out which values are dominant.

Use your sensory acuity to:

Notice dominant processing channels – ask questions about how the person is visualising and what he/she is imagining. Be specific about the location, size and clarity of their mental images. Is the visualisation followed by some other processing channel such as internal dialogue or feeling?

Establish dominant metaprogrammes and combinations of metaprogrammes and how they affect success.

Use the alignment model to:

Check for congruence at every level.

Strategies

Elicit any strategies which go to make up the model – for example, you may want to be able to handle setbacks in the same way as your subject. Elicit the thinking patterns and behaviours in detail.

What to do next

Once you are sure you have a complete and detailed model, you can decide whether this is something you would like to have. Be sure that you are congruent with every aspect of the model. For example, if you discover that, to achieve success, family sacrifices are made you need to be absolutely sure that this is OK for you.

Taking on the model

Having decided you would like this model first check your degree of congruence at every level of the Alignment model. Do this by placing markers on the floor to represent each of the levels and ask yourself the following questions while standing on the relevant marker. Write your answers here before proceeding to the next marker.

▶

Purpose – What do I want this model for? Is my purpose strong enough to make the necessary lifestyle changes this model will require?

_____

_____

_____

Identity – What will it be like to take on this new identity? Am I happy with how this will affect my other relationships – family, friends, colleagues, associates?

_____

_____

_____

Values and beliefs – Can I take on all of these without compromise?

_____

_____

_____

Capability – Have I got what it takes to learn and practise the new skills required by the model? Which skills and attitudes will I need?

_____

_____

_____

Behaviour – What changes will I be making to the things that I do on a regular basis? What opportunities can I generate for myself to practise?

_____

_____

_____

Environment – What impact will adopting this new model have on the rest of my life? Can I live with these changes?

_____

_____

_____

Once you are happy you are fully aligned with your intention to take on the new model, you can take a closer look at the specific changes. If you need to change some beliefs, use the techniques described in this book to help you – **fast belief change** or **precision questioning** technique. If you need to collapse some negative beliefs, use the **collapsing anchors** or **swish** technique. Visualise yourself being successful, creating clear, bright pictures associated with a positive tone of voice to demonstrate your conviction. Use the **new behaviour generator** technique to create new behaviours for yourself and really see yourself doing them.

Mentally test out your new model on other people by using the **Perceptual Positions** exercise.

Solo. Take your time as you stand on each marker to cover the full scope of each of the questions.

Duo. Use your sensory acuity to help the explorer break through the barriers and create powerful visions of behaving and thinking in this new way.

CHAPTER 11

From perception
to rules

Davina's story

Tom: 'Davina, when we were kids at school you were a real dare devil – into dangerous sports and always wearing bandages from some accident or other. You told me you wanted to take part in the Olympics one day doing something that everyone would admire you for because it was perceived as dangerous. Yet here you are with two children, a nice home, an excellent job and a secure lifestyle. What happened?'

Davina: 'I know, I can still remember the exhilaration of jumping off mountains on skis and diving into deep pools off the edge of the cliffs. When my Dad left I had to look after Sally and Ben while Mum worked. We never had any spare cash and Mum was constantly worried about us. I made up my mind that if ever I had children they would be able to have the experiences I had but with financial security as well.'

▶ brilliant overview

You are about to learn:

- People make rules for themselves and act according to their rules.
- There are unwritten rules formed by societies.
- Sometimes rules may serve you well and other times limit your potential.
- Rules can be changed.

▶

- Self-formed and societal rules form the framework for both your behaviour and your lifestyle.
- Personal change often requires a willingness to break out of societal rules and change your lifestyle.
- How to reframe your rules.
- How to take into account other people's perspectives.

Rules

Depending on what happens to us in life, we make either conscious or unconscious rules for ourselves which may or may not limit our potential. In previous chapters you have been working with the language patterns that indicate an underlying value or belief. The rules we make for ourselves are the result of adhering to such values and beliefs and are the framework we put around our behaviour. This framework determines our lifestyle which to a great extent defines who we are. When we are considering change we often need to accept a bigger change to our lifestyle than we might imagine. When personal change begins to impinge on our social lifestyle we may need to consider the ecology of such a change at the outset.

If you find your health deteriorating in any way, perhaps through lack of exercise, over-indulgence in food or too much passive activity like watching TV or computer games, or being a workaholic, attending to your situation will require a change of lifestyle. In close social groups sometimes your friends can react negatively to any sign of change as this could upset the cohesion in the group. One of the choices you may be faced with is whether your life is more important than the cohesion of a group you have been associated with. At times change can require breaking away from a group.

Here are some of the life rules that Davina set for herself:

- Get a 'steady' job so that I can support myself come what may.
- Make sure the children have a happy, stable upbringing.
- Keep Tom happy so that he stays with the family.
- Work hard and keep my head down at work.

- Make sure the children get everything I didn't have – holidays, clubs, etc.
- Keep fit and healthy by eating properly and exercising in the gym.
- Always have eight hours sleep when working the next day.
- Only drink alcohol at weekends.
- Never visit the supermarket without a list.
- Tuesday evening is housework evening.
- Sundays are for the children.
- Save carefully for a rainy day.
- Never borrow money.
- The house and garden must always look pristine in case someone calls.
- I value my friendship with the 'working women's lunch club' which meets once a month on a Saturday lunchtime.

Most of the time these rules worked well for Davina; sometimes the rigidity with which she stuck to them kept her constrained within her comfort zone and stifled her creativity.

Davina held strong values and beliefs supporting these rules which were created at childhood. Her parents' divorce had given her a strong value around family unity and the rules she set for herself mainly stemmed from this. Who can say whether her life would have taken a different course if her parents had stayed together or if she had reacted differently to the break-up?

Your rules help form your unique 'map of the world' from which you make choices and decisions of how to interact with the world. Remember that it is only a map – it isn't real, it's a set of mental perceptions; it's your way of navigating the complexity of the world you find yourself in. Your mental perceptions include your memories, judgements you have made, and beliefs you have built up. Your rules emerge from these perceptions. Personal change comes as a result of changing your personal map.

Personal rules

Here are some examples of personal rules which we have come across –
some quite common, others less so.

- I never fly long distance.
- I never associate with people who smoke.
- I never go out walking after dark.
- I have to do all DIY/motor repairs myself.
- I will only run for 10 minutes at a time.
- I never attend parties where I don't know anyone.
- I will check everyone out before I trust them.
- I will only do as much as I need to at work.
- I must eat three meals a day.
- Friday night is night out with the boys.
- I eat fish on Fridays.
- I research purchases over £50 in shops and on the internet.
- I check my bank account online every single day.
- I never buy expensive clothes or go on expensive holidays
- I only wear clothes of a certain type.
- I never wear a tie or a suit.
- I read the newspaper from cover to cover every day.
- I never miss the main evening news bulletin.
- I must wear brown shoes and socks with brown clothes.
- I must have a shower before I go out every day.
- I can't eat before I run.
- I will never be late for an appointment.
- I must stay married to my partner regardless.
- I don't accept things at face value.
- I will only live in this country.
- I never let people down.
- I must pursue education at all costs.
- I go to bed at 10.00 p.m. every night.

exercise 11.1 Testing the validity of your rules

What personal rules have you made for yourself? Make a list of all those you can bring to mind. You might not be able to think of them all now, so add them to the list as they occur to you at any time.

1 _____

2 _____

3 _____

4 _____

5 _____

6 _____

7 _____

8 _____

9 _____

10 _____

Now choose three that you feel could be limiting you or even if they are not challenge them anyway to test if they are still relevant. Ask yourself the following questions of each one:

1 Where did the rule originate from?

_____

2 What values and beliefs are supporting this rule?

_____

3 Is this rule still valid all of the time?

_____

4 If not, when is it valid?

_____

5 When is it not valid?

_____

6 Under what circumstances does this rule help you?

_____

▶

7 Under what circumstances might it be holding you back?

_____

8 What could happen if you broke the rule?

_____

9 What could happen if you changed the rule?

_____

10 Do other people have the same rule? If so, who?

_____

11 How does it work for them?

_____

12 What might be a more productive rule to have?

_____

13 Alternatively, would it be OK to drop the rule altogether?

_____

 **brilliant** action

Rules form the framework for your behaviour and lifestyle, and can either help or hinder you. What do your rules do for you? What do they do for other people? Are there any rules that you are unhappy with? If so, what would you like to change?

Societal rules

Mark was waiting in a queue at an airport. The queue was slow moving and so he wondered what he could do to pass the time. He decided to do some press-ups and stretching exercises on the floor. This had two benefits – one, that he got to take some exercise before getting on the plane; and two, being below the smoke level. You can imagine the curious looks from people passing by, and in the queue, as this is generally not considered *normal* queue behaviour. But who has got it right here? Those people who are conforming to the norm or Mark who dares to be different, stay out of the smoke, and get some exercise at the same time?

Pat was staying in a hotel while training. The hotel was a small family run hotel and the only one of its type in the area. As she was having dinner, she watched a group of elderly people gather at the bar. From their conversation this was a regular Wednesday evening event and an opportunity for these people to get dressed up and have dinner together. As the waiter indicated that dinner was being served, each lady took the arm of a gentleman and carefully walked the length of the dining room to their table at the far end. On reaching the table, one lady, who had been one of the slower walkers with a slight limp, realised she had left her drink in the bar and strode back at a fast pace to retrieve it. So what was the societal rule which led to the behaviour about being elderly here?

We have plenty to tell us we are getting old in the West – bus passes at the age of 60, statutory retirement age, concessionary entry into public events. In the East there are communities who view age very differently, referring to the years of 60 plus as the sage years to be admired and sought after, working and fathering children well into their nineties.

exercise 11.2 Societal rules

What societal rules can you think of that are either helping or restricting you/your colleagues/your community? Write them down here.

_____

_____

_____

_____

_____

_____

_____

_____

▶

What purpose do they serve and are they holding you back in any way?

_____

_____

_____

_____

_____

_____

Solo. This is a simple exercise to do alone – bear in mind that you will only focus on the aspects of your behaviour of which you are consciously aware. You may have unconscious behaviours that other people notice.

Duo. Give feedback to the explorer about rules you have noticed that may be outside his/her conscious awareness. Discuss these and describe what you see and hear the explorer doing and saying.

brilliant tip

Your mind has two modes of thought, conscious and unconscious. The trick is to use your conscious awareness with more focus, and to develop more productive thoughts in the unconscious mode. Begin by being more aware of your conscious mode and using it with positive intention to pursue fulfilling outcomes.

Reframing your perspective

Your rules will give you a unique perspective on life. In some contexts this perspective may serve you well and in others not so well. The way you interpret your perspective may be limiting you. If this is the case you can change the rule by reframing the perspective.

The reframe describes how behaviour which is perceived as 'against my rules' might actually be useful. For example, a rule about the behaviour of your teenage children may go something like 'they must be in at 10 p.m.

every night'. When your daughter complains and rebels you may form a perspective that 'she is so stubborn and wants her own way', insisting that she sticks to the rules. This may not be good for the relationship between the two of you. However, when being led astray by someone unscrupulous, you may appreciate the fact that she can be very stubborn and wants her own way. So the new perspective becomes: 'I am so pleased my daughter has a mind of her own and can be stubborn rather than weak-willed; it's not that she is stubborn, it's that she is growing up and learning to be her own person.'

exercise 11.3 Reframing your perspective

Revisit the rules you have listed in the previous exercise and assess the perspectives you have as a result of these rules. Where they limit you in any way come up with a reframe that could serve you more productively. Write your results here.

_____

_____

_____

_____

_____

_____

Solo. This is a simple exercise to do alone but sometimes you can miss obvious or more unconscious perspectives.

Duo. Help the explorer to reframe their perspectives by using the metamodel questions from Chapter 4 and offering suggestions for reframes.

Taking other people's perspectives

Conflict occurs when people defend their rules come what may. Whenever you are finding it difficult to communicate an idea, or to influence someone it is useful to try to see things from their perspective. Here is an exercise to help you understand and respect the rules someone else is using. You can then use their rules to build rapport and pace and lead the person towards your well-formed outcome.

 exercise 11.4 Perceptual positions

1   Decide who it is you would like to influence and imagine yourself in the exact location where this is likely to take place. For example, if you want to influence your manager to take on an idea, then you may imagine yourself in his/her office.

2   Physically set a scene using chairs and tables if appropriate to represent the physical environment as closely as possible. Decide where you will be sitting or standing and where your manager will be sitting or standing.

3   You are now going to look at the scenario from three different perspectives – 1 your own, 2 your manager's, and 3 as a fly on the wall looking back at the other two perspectives.

4   Position yourself on your make-believe set in the position where you will be in the real scenario, facing your manager and ask yourself the following questions:

   ● What is my purpose for doing this?

   ● What do I believe about this scenario?

   ● What is important to me about it?

   ● What do I want to happen as a result of this interaction?

5   When you have explored as much as you can from this position, move to where your manager will be sitting so that you are looking back at 'you'. Ask yourself the same questions as though you are now your manager. When you have fully explored this perspective, move to a place away from the scene where you can see both positions.

6   This is the fly on the wall perspective where you can learn the most from the interaction. From here compare your results from the questions you asked in the first two positions and ask yourself if there is anything you can do differently to ensure your outcome.

7   Revisit any position to clarify your learning and redefine your outcome if necessary.

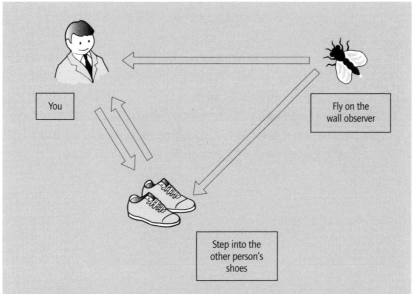

Solo. Although you can do this exercise alone, it is often more powerful if you gain the assistance of an NLP practitioner to ask you the appropriate questions and explore areas you may not be consciously aware of.

Duo. Stand beside the explorer in each position and use your sensory acuity to determine whether the answers are congruent and to tease out any limiting beliefs. Deal with whatever the explorer gives you if you feel there is room for a belief change or a reframe.

Whatever change of perception or behaviour you want to make, check the ecology using the four Cartesian logic questions in Chapter 1, and set yourself well-formed outcomes. Then make sure you have everything covered by asking these three big questions:

1 Are you willing and prepared to face the consequences of a lifestyle change in order to further your personal growth?

2 Are you willing and prepared to be seen as different by your social group when you make a change?

3 Have you factored in all the ecological aspects of making your change, and visualised your future having made the change?

Three yes's are all you need. We wish you every success.

CHAPTER 12

NLP's own belief system

> **It's all in the outlook: Seb and Carl's story**
>
> Carl: 'Come on, Seb, let's see if we can get these people to back
> us in this venture. We need financial support, some materials and
> some volunteers to run the programme.'
>
> Seb: 'Carl, it's never going to work, you can't trust people to do
> things and no-one is going to give us the money. Even if they did,
> you'd have to watch your back because they would have a hold
> over you.'

 **overview**

You are about to learn:

- That the way you approach life is based on a series of choices
- That NLP gives you more choices
- That there are beliefs upon which NLP is founded
- How life differs when you choose to either take on the beliefs or reject them.

brilliant examples

NLP is based upon a set of beliefs, called presuppositions, which are listed below.

For each presupposition you will be invited to choose a personal example. When you
have read them all and found examples for each, go back over the presuppositions
and imagine what it would be like to believe the opposite of each one.

The presuppositions of NLP

These presuppositions are not necessarily true, and they are offered to you as a choice, but when taken on board you are more likely to be successful at whatever you put your mind to.

Here they are identified with the letter P for presupposition.

P1: The map is not the territory

We each understand the world in our own way, and how we perceive it isn't how it actually is. We never have ALL the information ALL the time – and just as a map doesn't show every single house, shop, tree or bump in the road, our own maps are merely our own representation of the world, rather than reality, or the territory. We create our maps by filtering information through our senses, the language we use, metaprogrammes, our beliefs and values and our experience.

This is why Carl and Seb were able to create such differing perceptions. Carl was filtering for positive experiences while Seb was filtering for the negative ones.

In Chapter 10 you learnt that you make rules for yourself. These rules become part of your reality and therefore your map. You have probably begun to challenge some of these already. Here is an opportunity for you to challenge some more.

exercise 12.1 People watching

Take some time to watch people around you who you know something about and who are in similar circumstances to yourself. Are they successful in areas where you aren't? What beliefs do they hold that differ from your own and could be having an impact on their success? Record your findings here.

_____

_____

_____

_____

Solo. When you find someone doing something that you would like to do, ask them questions about their approach, what is important to them and what they believe about their ability to succeed.

Duo. Use precision questioning to help the explorer identify what it is they would like to do. Help them identify people who have this skill and offer suggestions as to the questions they may ask to determine the thinking behind the skill.

P2: Respect others' maps of the world

As we each have a unique representation of reality, there can be no right or wrong map. It is important therefore to work with, and seek to understand, another person's map. By respecting others' maps, and acknowledging the differences instead of assuming one is right or wrong, we can gather more information and use this to build rapport, expand our own maps and build more successful relationships. Respect does not mean you have to agree. Learn to be curious rather than judgemental.

exercise 12.2 From judgement to curiosity

Think of the last time you judged someone or something only to discover that your judgement wasn't useful. Write it down here.

_____

_____

_____

Now write down what you could have thought had you decided to be curious rather than judgemental.

_____

_____

_____

▶

Having expanded your thinking, how might your behaviour have differed had you been curious rather than judgemental?

_____

_____

_____

_____

_____

P3: The meaning of your communication is in the response

Take responsibility for your own communication and the effect it has. If someone reacts in a way you weren't anticipating, or takes a different meaning from the one you wanted to communicate, you can ask yourself: 'How else can I explain, say or do this?' It would be all too easy to say, 'It's not my fault, he just didn't listen' or 'This is a really difficult group of students, they don't take on board anything I say.'

exercise 12.3 Check how you respond to different people

Think about the people who you are happy to do things for. How do they communicate with you? How do you respond?

_____

_____

_____

_____

Now think about the people you resent doing things for. How do they communicate and how do you respond?

_____

_____

_____

_____

P4: If it's possible for one person, it's possible for others

People have all the inner resources they need to make a change. There are no unresourceful people, only unresourceful states of mind. Those who excel at something are using strategies and states that work well.

When you hear some of the following phrases they are usually an indication of limited thinking in relation to possibility:

- *It's all right for him because ...*
- *I'll never be able to do that because ...*
- *If only I could ...*
- *If I had enough money/time/resources I would be able to ...*
- *He can do that because he has ...*

exercise 12.4 Personal limitation audit

Write down any limitations you may be putting on yourself in this way. Keep this section at the front of your mind and note down any limitation you catch yourself voicing over the next few weeks. Keep a running list for a complete audit of the limitations you catch yourself saying.

_____

_____

_____

_____

_____

P5: There is no failure, only feedback

If what you do doesn't create the desired result, you have still created a result. Use the feedback to explore what you can do differently to get the outcome you want. Ask yourself: 'What can I learn from this?' and 'What can I do differently?' Focus on solutions and what else is possible rather than problems.

Thomas Edison didn't wake up one morning and decide to put a light bulb in a socket. His invention took time and many 'failed' attempts before people were able to flick a light switch instead of lighting a candle. Computer programmers don't get it right first time – the existence of beta versions of new programs tells us that they are work in progress.

Everything we do is a learning experience from which we can gain valuable insight and feedback ready for the next time we attempt something similar.

exercise 12.5 **Feedback**

Think of the last time you perceived yourself to have 'failed'. What action did you take as a result? Did you try again or did you give up and say 'this is not for me – I am no good at this'? If you were to try again what would you do differently?

_____

_____

_____

_____

P6: Mind and body are part of the same system

Behaviour includes thinking as well as actions, both physical and verbal. All behaviour is the result of thinking and feeling a certain way. If you feel bad about something, and you would rather not, then change your thinking and change your posture.

exercise 12.6 **Courage**

Think of something you would really like to do but haven't yet found the courage. How would your thinking have to change in order for you to take the first steps?

_____

_____

_____

_____

P7: Every behaviour has a positive intention

People make the best choices they can with the resources they have available at the time. The positive intention may not always be apparent. One person may shout and scream at another, and the positive intention behind the screaming is to help the screamer feel they are taking control. A positive intention doesn't necessarily have a positive result.

exercise 12.7 Guess the positive intent

Here are some perceived negative behaviours. What do you think could be the positive intention behind them? Of course, you are only guessing here. Without a real example, it is impossible to know for sure, but attempting to answer this question will give you an insight into the concept.

● Shouting at a loved one because 'they smiled at someone else', 'didn't do something you asked them to' or 'said something unpleasant'.

_____

_____

● Stopping a child from going out to play with his friends.

_____

_____

● Getting drunk, smoking or taking drugs.

_____

_____

● Telling a friend or colleague you don't like something or someone.

_____

_____

● Overeating.

_____

_____

▶

● Showing off.

_____

_____

● Blaming something which is your responsibility on to someone else.

_____

_____

● Finding an excuse for not doing something you promised to do.

_____

_____

P8: The person with the most flexibility will have most control

Use flexibility of thinking and behaviour to understand the other person's map of the world, build rapport and achieve outcomes. Being fixed and rigid can create a stalemate situation where no desired outcomes are achieved. If you are rigid, you have limited choices as to 'how' to approach something. Having flexibility is being open to try other ways of succeeding.

exercise 12.8 Flexibility

Think of someone you come into contact with regularly but find difficult to understand. Make a list of all the things they do well.

_____

_____

_____

_____

_____

Knowing what you know about visual, auditory and kinaesthetic processing and metaprogrammes what can you ascertain is the basis for their success? What else do you know about them that makes them successful in this area?

_____
_____
_____
_____
_____

How can you flex your behaviour to improve your chances of communicating more effectively?

_____
_____
_____
_____

When will you take the first step?

_____
_____

P9: If you always do what you've always done, you'll always get what you've always had

We tend to repeat patterns of behaviour even though we are aware they are not working for us. Until we learn to re-programme our thinking and habits our results won't change.

How often have you said to yourself, 'I really must ...' then started it and gave up only to start again some time later? How many times have you repeated this pattern? This is usually because you are trying to change something at the level of behaviour – refer back to the neurological levels model in Chapter 5. In order for change to happen you will need to make a change at a higher level – perhaps you don't have the skills yet, or your beliefs and values are out of alignment, or maybe you don't see yourself as 'the type of person who does this' or maybe you haven't managed to establish clarity around your purpose for doing it.

exercise 12.9 Aligning to change

Think of something you have made several attempts at changing in yourself – your weight, an irritating habit, an aggressive approach, inability to say 'no', indecision, compulsive buying or something else.

_____

_____

_____

_____

_____

_____

Refer to the neurological levels model in Chapter 5 and ask yourself where the misalignment occurs. Go through each level one at a time and only ask yourself questions related to that level. Space some cards representing each level on the floor equidistant apart and ask the questions below as you stand on each card:

● What is my purpose for making this change?

● How will this change alter my sense of who I am?

● What is important to me about making this change?

● What do I believe will happen if I make this change?

● What do I believe will happen if I don't make this change?

● What do I believe won't happen if I make this change?

● What do I believe won't happen if I don't make this change?

● What skills will I need to make this change?

● How will I achieve these skills?

● What impact will this change have on those around me?

● When will I make this change?

How to get the most out of this exercise

Solo. Do the exercise standing up. Place the cards representing each level on the floor equidistant apart and move between them, only asking the questions relating to each level as you move from level to level. Feel free to revisit any that you perceive to require more clarity. When you have extracted the learning, stand on the purpose card and imagine yourself having achieved your purpose. What can you see, hear and feel?

Duo. Set the exercise up as for 'Solo'. Use your sensory acuity and precision questioning to ascertain whether you feel the answers are congruent. Feel free at any stage to help the explorer using any of the NLP techniques in this book.

P10: A person's behaviour is not who they are

Behaviour is something people do – it is not who they are. Have you ever watched someone doing something harsh and wondered what on earth makes them do that? Chances are if you dig deep there will be a positive intention. Maybe the harshness is a form of protection against previous hurt, covering a softness the person is afraid to reveal for fear of being hurt again.

Remember also that you only ever see part of the person. In order to see the whole spectrum of a person's behaviour you would have to be with them 24 hours a day seven days a week. People behave differently in different scenarios so there is always a possibility that a person behaves differently when you are not around. Also people do change their behaviour.

P11: Your perception is your reality

Your own perceived reality is created by the way you filter information. Two people experiencing the same situation will have different perceptions of it. For example, a referee watching a football match may be watching the performance of the referee whereas an avid fan of one of the teams may be watching the performance of one particular player. Both are watching the same match but may come away with a different account of their experience depending on the referee's performance and whether or not the team won the match.

Your focus of interest will play a part in your own reality. Two people, one with a focus of interest on location and the other on people, will have a different experience entering a room full of people for the first time. One will look around at the décor and the other will focus on who is in the room.

On the basis that no two people can possibly have exactly the same experience there are very few universal truths. Again curiosity is the key here – being curious about other people's maps will give you more information upon which to act and help increase your flexibility.

P12: I'm in charge of my mind and, therefore, my results

If we are in control of our thoughts, we are in control of our behaviour and, therefore, responsible for our results. Refer to the model of communication in Chapter 10 for a greater insight into this presupposition. You can test this for yourself.

exercise 12.10 **Connecting the mind with a desired result**

Write down something you believe wholeheartedly about someone close to you.

_____

_____

_____

_____

Now imagine what it would be like to believe the opposite.

_____

_____

_____

_____

Each belief will have an impact on your behaviour towards this person – you have a choice as to which one to believe – you are in control. Run through this exercise again using a belief about yourself, or about an aspect of your work which you really enjoy. The more you test out your beliefs, the more you will realise how much your results rely upon the way you are thinking, and that making a change is actually very easy to do.

P13: Resistance is a sign of a lack of rapport

If you are experiencing resistance from someone, it shows that rapport is lacking and a satisfactory outcome is unlikely.

Think back to the last major purchase you made which involved communicating with a sales person – maybe a new car or a bathroom or kitchen. How did you feel about the person you were negotiating with? Did you trust them; like them; feel they had your best interests at heart? Conversely, think about a purchase you would like to have made but didn't because the sales person irritated you in some way.

We often meet people who undervalue what they refer to as 'small talk', viewing it as trivial and unnecessary. We always offer them a reframe. 'Small talk' is the essential rapport building stage that is going to put you into a position of influence, whatever it is you are trying to achieve. Without it you are unlikely to succeed. We encourage you to think of it as 'big talk' not 'small talk'.

P14: A person cannot not communicate

Even sitting quietly with an 'expressionless' face communicates something. There has been a lot written about body language and what it means. Consequently, it is very easy to create a false meaning about body language:

- *He is tapping his foot, he must want to get away.*
- *He has his arms crossed, he is being defensive.*
- *She is looking out of the window, she is not interested in what I am saying.*

- *He is lounging back in his chair, he is very sloppy.*
- *Her face is screwed up, she must be cross.*

How will making one of these judgements affect your behaviour towards these people? There is of course the possibility that each of these statements may be true and an equal possibility that they are not. We know from our learning so far that people will sit or stand in a manner which assists their filtering and processing channels. For example, gazing out of the window could mean the person is processing what you have said visually and needs the distance the window offers to do so. Lounging in a chair is a common trait of someone with a kinaesthetic processing channel, as is crossing arms.

Remember that you will be giving off signals that others will interpret in some way. Much has been written about the meaning of body language and depending on which books someone has read they will be attaching meanings to your body language. Make sure you use your sensory acuity here and use your physiology to build rapport.

P15: People have all the resources they need to change

On the basis that we all have the ability to think and act for ourselves, making changes to our thinking will have a consequential impact on our behaviour. We often hear this referred to as latent or hidden potential. The job of an NLP practitioner is to help the explorer access their inner resources.

 **action**

When you have completed the exercises in this chapter, take another look at the presuppositions and imagine what it would be like to believe the opposite of each one.

Index of exercises

Index

the brilliant series

Fast and engaging, the *Brilliant* series works hard to make sure you stand out from the crowd. Each *Brilliant* book has been carefully crafted to ensure everything you read is practical and applicable – to help you make a difference now.

9780273724902

Stephen Briers

brilliant
Cognitive Behavioural Therapy

9780273732556

Dave Melden & Pat Hutchinson

brilliant
NLP

2nd Edition

What the most successful people know, do and say

9780273735885

Mike McClement

brilliant
Confidence

How to challenge your fears and go for anything you want in life

9780273740742

Max Eggert

brilliant
Body Language

How to understand and interpret our secret signals

9780273740544

Mike Clayton

brilliant
Influence

What the most influential people know, do and say

9780273737438

David Molden

brilliant
NLP
Workbook

Practical tips, techniques and tools to harness the power of NLP

9780273743224

Anne Lionnet

brilliant
Life Coach

10 inspirational steps to transform your life

2nd Edition

9780273738213

Charlotte Style

brilliant
Positive Psychology

What makes us happy, optimistic and motivated

9780273744092

Mike Clayton

brilliant
Time Management

What the most productive people know, do and say

9780273723271

Nic Peeling

brilliant
Retirement

Everything you need to know and do to make the most of your golden years

9780273724933

Emma Sargent

brilliant
Parent

What the best parents know, do and say

9780273718338

Anne Lionnet

brilliant
Relationships

Your ultimate guide to creating happy and fulfilling relationships

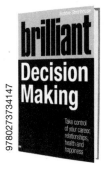

9780273734147
9780273714804
9780273743217
9780273730675
9780273722328
9780273743231
9780273720591
9780273717355
9780273726463
9780273725114
9780273721239
9780273712350

Whatever your level, we'll get you to the next one.
It's all about you. Get ready to shine!